SPRINGS *of* WATER *in a* DRY LAND

SPRINGS *of* WATER *in a* DRY LAND

Spiritual Survival

for Catholic

Women Today

MARY JO WEAVER

Beacon Press • *Boston*

Beacon Press
25 Beacon Street
Boston, Massachusetts 02108-2892

Beacon Press books
are published under the auspices of
the Unitarian Universalist Association of Congregations.

99 98 97 96 95 94   8 7 6 5 4 3 2

Text design by Linda Koegel

Earlier versions of some of the chapters in this book appeared in the following
publications: portions of the preface in an essay in *Listening: Journal of Religion
and Culture* 25 (Winter 1990), pp. 86–101; "Called to a New Land" in *New
Woman, New Church: Newsletter of the Women's Ordination Conference*; "Springs of
Water in a Dry Land" in *A Discipleship of Equals: Towards a Christian Feminist
Spirituality*, vol. XX of the *Proceedings of the Theology Institute of Villanova Uni-
versity*; and "Who Is the Goddess and Where Does She Get Us?" in *Journal of
Feminist Studies in Religion* 5 (Spring 1989) and in Mary Ellen Brown, ed., *New
Paganism: A Feminist Search for Religious Alternatives*, Occasional Series no. 3,
Women's Studies Program (Bloomington: Indiana University, 1988), pp. 3–
24. All are reprinted by permission.

Library of Congress Cataloging-in-Publication Data

Weaver, Mary Jo.
    Springs of water in a dry land : spiritual survival for Catholic
women today / Mary Jo Weaver.
        p.   cm.
    Includes bibliographical references and index.
    ISBN 0-8070-1218-1 (cloth)
    ISBN 0-8070-1219-x (paper)
    1. Women, Catholic—Religious life.   2. Women in the Catholic
Church.   I. Title.
BX2353.W43   1993
282'.082—dc20   92-8036
                                                    CIP

FOR JEAN ALICE MCGOFF

CONTENTS

ACKNOWLEDGMENTS

I would like to thank the various groups that asked me to help them think about feminist spirituality by writing a paper for them. I probably would not have moved in this direction had it not been for invitations I could not refuse. The Women's Ordination Conference invited me to give the keynote address for their tenth anniversary (1985). An independent group of women in Portland, Oregon, headed by Cindy Barrett and Mary LeBarre provided the opportunity that eventually led to "Springs of Water in a Dry Land" (1987), an essay I later expanded for the Villanova Summer Theology Institute. One of my students, Garbo Todd, chagrined at my ignorance about neopaganism, inspired me to work with the women's studies program at Indiana University to design the conference at which I reflected on the Goddess (1989). The fiftieth anniversary of the establishment of the American branch of the Grail movement gave me an idea for an essay on Grail women as an alternative in community living (1990), and I am grateful to members of that group, especially to Janet Kalven, Audrey Sorrento, and Dan and Mary Kane. The University of Portland invited me to teach part of their summer school program in 1990 and asked for a public lecture as well. I wrote "At Home in Her Own House" for them and was delighted to renew old acquaintances and meet new friends. Barbara Wahl at Villanova asked me to write an essay on spirituality for women who work. This request threw me into a real quandary—since *all* women work—but finally led me to "Spiritual Work" (1991), for which I am deeply grateful. Since I believe that I think best in images, I am grateful for those opportunities to imagine new pictures or to tell new stories. My talks to various groups of sisters around the country and my participation in Womenchurch conferences and workshops have led me to think about new chapels, new lands, and the desert, which is the context for this book and its final word.

I have tried out some of these ideas on two good friends, Anne Carr and Joann Wolski Conn, because they are critical in an unfailingly positive way. When I have been stuck and anxious about *starting* an essay, I have relied on a constant source of intellectual energy, Susan Gubar, and have never been disappointed. Marianna Bridge was a steady support and a good reader. I am grateful to my editors and proofreaders, to Carlisle Rex-Waller and Erin Cornish, and especially to Alice Falk. I owe special thanks to Lauren Bryant of Beacon Press for her guidance, clarity, and dedicated support.

Finally, however, this book owes its life to those who shape my spiritual journey. Jean Alice McGoff and her sisters have helped me to understand the little I know about Teresa of Avila and John of the Cross and have made my learning experiences a pleasure. Jean Alice in particular has seen me through my own difficult times, guiding me to the odd oasis, pointing to an occasional flower in what I thought was a pretty bleak landscape. I dedicate this book to her with great pleasure and affection.

FOUR STORIES

In my earlier study of feminism and Catholicism, *New Catholic Women* (San Francisco: Harper and Row, 1985), I wondered if the phrase "Catholic feminist" were oxymoronic. How could one hold on to one side of this self-definition without betraying the other? How could one relinquish one aspect or the other and still be faithful to one's identity? Nearly ten years later, Roman Catholicism still looks bleak from a feminist perspective: the language of the liturgy, the politics of ordination, the negative attitudes toward women, the inadequate pastoral responses to wrenching problems like birth control, abortion, and abuse all have given women more than enough reasons to leave their church. Nevertheless, from a believer's perspective, Catholicism holds many attractions: the beauty of the liturgy, the call to ordination experienced by many women, positive or hopeful stories about women in the church, and the willingness of great numbers of women to continue to struggle *as Catholics* with vexing moral problems like birth control, abortion, and abuse all have given some feminists more than enough reasons to stay in their church.

Decisions to stay within institutional Catholicism or to go from it, however satisfying they might be on a practical level, are often troublesome emotionally. A woman who has in some way solved the affiliation problem for herself has often not resolved deeper religious questions. Does a decision to remain within the church mean acceptance of all official teachings and satisfaction with traditional symbols and forms of spirituality? Does a decision to leave the institution mean a formal abandonment of the religious quest and a general dismissal of religion as an important component of one's life? These questions cannot be easily answered. My work with Catholic women suggests that many of them yearn for a different approach to spirituality precisely because they hold both aspects of a Catholic feminist identity dear. Those still "within" the church struggle to integrate a feminist perspective into their religious lives while those "outside" of it, however glibly they may describe themselves as "recovering Catholics," continue to be shaped by their reactions to their backgrounds. Inside or outside the institution, Catholic feminists hunger for spiritual nourishment and attempt to find religiously enriching conversation and dynamic opportunities for spiritual growth.

As I have talked with Catholic women over the past ten years, I have heard stories of profound dislocation from women of all ages and in a variety of circumstances. Reduced to the simplest terms, many Catholic women find themselves in a double bind: living with misogyny and oppressive institutional structures is torture, but rejecting a church suffused with rich spiritual symbolism and a sacramental reality is starvation. What can such women do?

To engage these problems as concretely as possible, I have created a set of characters who reflect the experiences of many American Catholic women. My four prototypes are composite characters; they show how the lives of individual women have led to a marked increase in feminist consciousness on the part of many American Catholic women. And they raise the questions that, in one way or another, I have tried to grapple with throughout the essays in this book.

Mary O'Donnell

Mary O'Donnell, born in the Midwest in 1920, is a second-generation Irish Catholic who married her childhood sweetheart in 1942. Although Mary was taught, and theoretically believed, that women should find total fulfillment in marriage and family, she did not. When her third child was born four years after her marriage, she urged her husband, Tom, to think about birth control. He told her he would talk to their pastor, and she was not surprised that the church's answer to her problem was a rehearsal of traditional Catholic teaching about the glories of motherhood and the evils of birth control. Three miscarriages and four additional children put an enormous strain on the marriage. She was frazzled. He was drained. As she became overworked and depressive, he was increasingly absent, sometimes working overtime and sometimes just out. When he was home, he was abusive verbally and physically. In this unhappy situation, the children began to have problems. When Mary consulted her pastor about the situation, he directed her to the lives of the saints and urged her to find salvation through suffering.

As the children got older, everything Mary had held dear began to collapse. Her oldest daughter married a Protestant and practiced birth control. Tom Jr., bitter and confused about celibacy, left the seminary after his deacon year in order to get married. Mary's marriage appeared to be unredeemable, and the Second Vatican Council unsettled her conviction that the Catholic church would never change. After painful consideration, she divorced Tom, moved away, and began a quiet reflective life of her own. If she was angry with the church, she never said so. She retreated to a pre-Vatican II devotional Catholicism that was a comfort to her.

When the pope visited the United States in 1979, Mary managed to get to one of his appearances. Fretful about being a divorced Catholic, she ached for approval. His speech changed her life. She was expecting the Vicar of Christ to be Christlike, to preach mercy and forgiveness; but she heard harsh words condemning birth control and divorce. She went home shaken and two days later sat down to write a letter to the pope. Although she began with all due respect, she found herself overtaken by past agony and by her Irish temper. "Who the *hell* do you think you are?" she asked the pope with fury. "Jesus did not come to condemn people. What do *you* know about real life anyway?" What kind of institution preached love in the abstract, she wondered?

The letter, which she sent to her daughter, but not to the pope, was cleansing. Sensing that she would not find what she wanted from the Vicar of Christ, she began to look for it elsewhere. In her search for meaning, she became interested in the women's movement and joined a conversation in her church that was supposed to share women's needs with the bishops. In the discussion sessions, she was bold: "What is wrong with women's ordination?" Many of the women in her parish wanted the bishops to consider married priests, divorce, and birth control. The pastor, looking over the list of "women's concerns," shook his head sadly. "No matter," thought Mary O'Donnell. Sure of herself for the first time, she is now not so sure about the future of the Catholic church.

Elizabeth Miller

Elizabeth Miller, born in 1930, always felt especially loved by God and called to religious life. No one was surprised when she joined a contemplative order in 1950 to find salvation as a bride of Christ. In the convent of the Poor Clares, Elizabeth learned silence, mortification of the flesh, fasting, and the salvific possibilities of physical discomfort. Trained to find God's will in darkness, she nevertheless kept her mind open to new ideas. Under the direction of an enlightened prioress, she and her sisters read modern European theologians.

When the Second Vatican Council met in the early 1960s, Elizabeth was profoundly moved by it. She urged her sisters to take advantage of the freedom offered to nuns in the decree on religious life. When a group of contemplative sisters across the country began to talk to one another—a move unheard of just ten years earlier—she was part of the conversation. When this same group decided to sponsor a week-long series of talks and activities in Woodstock in 1969, Elizabeth was sent by her monastery despite a last-minute attempt on the part of some conservative bishops to discourage contemplative sisters from leaving their cloisters to attend meetings.

Woodstock changed her life. Elizabeth was invigorated by the conferences about the "new theology," the discussions of the classics of the contemplative tradition, and by her developing friendships with other cloistered nuns. She joined a new, officially unrecognized association that planned to hold seminars every two years. Her prayer life deepened as she practiced new forms of contemplation. When participants in the feminist movement began to question some of the church's teaching about women, she understood their questions and took courage from them.

Her monastery flourished. The sisters decided to remove the grilles and other barriers between themselves and the "outside world." Cloister was kept, but was understood as a state of mind and heart more than as a physically inhibiting structure. Little by little, the sisters became as enthusiastic about new forms of spirituality, feminism, and world religions as they were about the classics of the Catholic spiritual tradition.

Throughout the 1970s, the Vatican reacted to monasteries like Elizabeth's, telling the sisters who wanted to experiment that they should seek dismissal from their vows and lead a different life. Monastic legislation written in Rome demanded a return to the habit, a rebuilding of grilles, and strict observance of papal cloister. In order to comply with Vatican directives, Elizabeth would have to deny twenty years of positive experience. To continue the expansive spiritual journey she and her sisters have begun, to stay open to the power of the spirit in their lives, Elizabeth realizes that she must resist the institution that has been the center of her existence.

Annette Anderson

Annette Anderson was born in 1950. She attended Catholic schools and understood herself to be inexorably Catholic. In college she was in the Sodality of the Blessed Virgin Mary, went to daily mass, and was considered pious. Although attracted to convent life, she decided to work "in the world" as a single woman. She did not know what words to use to describe her decision, but she was sure that she did not want marriage, and she knew, on a barely conscious level, that she was attracted to women.

The 1970s were tumultuous years for Annette. Having initially resisted the changes of Vatican II, she became a convinced postconciliar Catholic. Fascinated with religion and understanding the potential of a truly ecumenical theology, she was accepted for doctoral work at the divinity school at the University of Chicago. She also began to cope with questions she had theretofore avoided. After a long personal struggle, she came to understand and accept herself as a lesbian. Her parents and siblings were neither terribly surprised nor particularly judgmental: they recognized Annette's love for the church and hoped, with her, that if she led a discreet life, she could still serve the interests of Catholicism with integrity.

As feminism emerged all around her, Annette joined a women's group. She became more thoroughly feminist in her outlook but no less enthralled with the study of religion. Indeed, she found herself longing for ordination. The Detroit Women's Ordination Conference in 1976 made her proud to be a Catholic feminist and she ardently hoped that priesthood would open up for her and other women she knew. She was prepared for it: she had a Ph.D. in theology, she was certified in clinical pastoral education, she had worked as a volunteer chaplain's assistant in a local hospital, she prayed with an ecumenical support group, and she loved the church.

When the Vatican decree against the ordination of women appeared in October 1976, she was hurt and angry. She demonstrated at diocesan ordinations in Chicago, worked in "ministerial" jobs with sympathetic priests, and tried to endure. By 1980, however, when it was clear to her that she would never be a priest, she left the Catholic church to join the Methodists. She was ordained in 1984 and sent to work in a large urban church. Although she was quite at home with the Methodist interest in social justice, she longed for a more formal liturgy. She missed frequent celebration of the Eucharist and felt that her change in religious affiliation was a high price to pay for ordination.

In 1985, Annette had a chance to go to Nicaragua as a missionary observer. That experience changed her life. She now works in an area where people need her liturgical skills. She is sometimes homesick for Catholicism, but in view of the 1986 Vatican decree against homosexuality, she says, not without regret, that there is no place in that church for her.[1] She says that she is happy to be where she is.

Patricia Reily

Patricia Reily, born in 1960, was reared in an enthusiastic Catholic family. Both her parents were active in her local parish, and Patty's religious life was idyllic: women were eucharistic ministers and lectors, girls as well as boys were acolytes, sermons were aimed at social justice, and fellow parishioners formed a real support community. When she went to a state university in California to study, she expected the same kind of lively Catholic atmosphere she had left behind, but the Newman Center was a chilling place with a preconciliar pastor and liturgy not very appealing to college students.

When she took a women's studies course, she found herself continually defending her Catholicism. "How can you be a Catholic feminist?" her friends wondered. "Haven't you read Mary Daly? Haven't you read your own tradition?" When she did read Daly, who in landmark studies like *The Church and the Second Sex* (Boston: Beacon Press, 1968) indicts the Catholic church as a sexist institution, she was shocked and confused. Daly's books made sense in the context of Patty's present experience, but surely, she thought, the Newman Center was an aberration. Surely her home parish was more typical. She resisted the critics and was thankful that in most places the Catholic church had progressed to the point where women's talents were respected.

In the middle of the semester of her freshman year, the Vatican issued a decree against the ordination of women. Patty was stunned. She knew about the birth control encyclical of the late 1960s, knew how people had ignored it and changed the practical policy of American Catholicism; but she did not see how this might work in the case of ordination. When she went home for Christmas, she talked to her parents about ordination and was not consoled to hear them warn that Catholicism moves slowly. Still, the local parish council had altered most of the language of the liturgy so that it was inclusive, women were very much in evidence on the altar, and one could hope that the visibility of women would stimulate real change.

In April, her mother wrote that they were getting a new pastor. He was young, which sounded promising, and Patty was eager for summer vacation. When she arrived home, however, she found herself spiritually homeless. The new pastor had been there only one month, and the parish had changed dramatically. The parish council had resigned *en masse* because the pastor continually abrogated their decisions. Female acolytes were now forbidden, women were invited to serve coffee rather than communion, sermons were, her parents told her, reminiscent of the 1950s. The language changes that had been operative in the parish were discontinued. Her parents were heartsick, her younger siblings totally uninterested in going to church.

When Patty returned to school in the fall, the situation at the Newman Center had not changed, but she had. Whereas before she had tried to persuade her disenchanted Catholic friends to stay open to the possibilities of a vibrant church by extolling her own background and parish, now she had little to say. It is not that she does not care. She cares very much. But where will she go?

There are many stories such as these. Although these characters are fictional, they describe people who have been caught up in a paradigm shift. All of these women were nurtured in the Catholic tradition: they accepted it, loved it, and attempted to build their lives around it. Yet when the circumstances of their lives changed, when their experience urged them to question the church or hope for something new, the tradition betrayed them.

Mary O'Donnell and Elizabeth Miller, born in the early part of this century, believed that they were part of an unchanging tradition. If Catholicism was unbending and difficult, that was simply a fact and salvation turned upon one's ability to conform to the teachings of the church. Both accepted the Catholic tradition without question, and neither of them would have been able to relate to the phrase, "We are the church," had it not been for the momentous shifts of Vatican II.

The Second Vatican Council disrupted Mary's religious life just when her married life was collapsing. Her retreat into old devotional patterns and her longing for some definitive word of mercy from the pope both testified to a need for understanding from an outside authority. Her letter to the pope was her way of claiming her own voice. If the church must change with the times, she reasoned, if it is bound to consider the real lives of its members, then her life and her thoughts were part of the life and mind of the church. Her daughter's acceptance of artificial birth control, her son's problems with clerical celibacy, her own dissolved marriage became part of her religious journey. Her faith in God and her confidence in herself enabled her to resist the marginalization that the Vatican seemed eager to impose on women in her position.

Unlike Mary, Elizabeth had been prepared for change. Her reading of modern theology and the strength of her communal life enabled her to adapt, and she accepted the teachings of Vatican II as eagerly as she had lived her preconciliar life. By the late 1960s, Elizabeth believed that she was part of a living tradition, that her experience counted for something in the economy of the church. Today she will neither accept old rules imposed without consultation nor leave a community with whom she has spent the past forty years. The insights of Vatican II, a belief in the spirit manifest in the life of the community, and a rich prayer life have made her into a quiet subversive.

Annette Anderson and Patty Reily were born into a fluid situation. The real glory of the Catholic church for each of them was its ability to adapt to changes, to welcome dialogue with members of other religions, and to be sensitive to the needs of the real world. Both were able to embrace postconciliar Catholicism eagerly, and both dreamed of the church as a living reality in which the best parts of the old tradition could blend with the needs of a new order.

Annette's acceptance of her homosexuality was made possible by the increasing willingness of American theologians to consider relational images of salvation and human interaction.[2] Her desire to become a priest was upheld by feminist theologians and hundreds of like-minded women for whom ordination seemed more than a remote fantasy. She felt betrayed by the Vatican's high-handed condemnation of women's ordination, hurt as much by the tone as by the teaching. The Vatican document on homosexuality further convinced her that her move to another denomination was for the best.

Patty had grown up in an exceptional parish that she mistook for normative Catholicism. She realizes now that a change in pastors can profoundly alter her own life. She hopes for a new pastor at the Newman Center, but she knows that such a solution will not address the problem for her after graduation. She does not want to live in fear of her spiritual future, but she does not know how to shape that future for herself.

For many American Catholic women, these composite life stories are true. Many Catholic women have been betrayed by a church they love. I have shaped the stories to reflect a sense of painful loss rather than anger in order to create portraits of hopefulness. It would be perfectly possible, however, and perhaps more honest, to recount stories of rage and anguish that have driven women out of the church. Many women who have left Catholicism are engaged in the exploration of religious alternatives, but many have abandoned Catholicism and religion altogether. Those who stay, attempting to hold on to their Catholic identity even as they affirm themselves as feminists, live in a painful space between hope and despair, nourishment and starvation.

In the interest of fairness, I should also have included women who are quite at home in Roman Catholicism as it is now, or as it existed before the council. Many of them, too, are angered and frustrated by the interactions between Roman Catholicism and feminism. Many perceive feminists as would-be destroyers of some of their most cherished beliefs and devotions, especially those relating to the Blessed Virgin Mary.

The pain and rage I have encountered in my work with Catholic women are mixed with many other emotions that shape the particularities of their individual lives. Underneath these primal feelings, however, there is longing for *place*. Some long for a physical space in which they can be spiritually nourished or celebrate the liturgy; others try to achieve internal composure, to find a state of mind that eases the tensions of maintaining a Catholic feminist identity; still others manage to find wellsprings of motivation to keep demonstrating and working for recognition of the justice of the feminist agenda. I myself long for an inner quiet where, as John of the Cross says, I can "be content with a loving and peaceful attentiveness to God" (*The Dark Night of the Soul*, book I, chap. 10). These places are hard to find, but they are well worth looking for. The essays that constitute this book are my attempt to articulate the longing for place that

I have found among a variety of Catholic women in America. Their yearning is rooted in their searches for meaningful spirituality in an often misogynist church.

I have written these essays over a long period of time with different audiences in mind. In many ways, they represent my own struggle to combine solid theoretical perspectives with pressing practical needs, but it will be clear to readers that my own interest lies more in stating the questions than in offering possible solutions to difficult problems. Definite answers to questions need to be wrestled with individually or collectively and will change with the circumstances of those involved. As a scholar of American Catholicism in general and the women's movement within the Catholic church in particular, I find that I am fascinated by different embodiments of spiritual perplexity, but am reluctant to suggest specific answers to the real questions of various groups.

I have tried to enter sympathetically into the different worlds I describe in this book and to avoid taking a particular viewpoint as if it were the only possible perspective. Although I was trained as a theologian to believe that my task was to articulate eternal truths in contemporary language, my professional life has been spent in a state university in a department of religious studies. I therefore believe my best work is done when I try to understand the differences that divide people. I am more interested in description than in persuasion, though I am quite willing to bring my own ideas into the conversation to see how well they resonate with the needs of a particular audience.

Many of these essays have been written since the publication of *New Catholic Women* and are full of the footnotes and apparatus that go along with new work. The talk I presented for the tenth anniversary of the Women's Ordination Conference—"Called to a New Land"—was written at about the same time that *New Catholic Women* was published. The arguments and ideas presented in the essay build on the research I did for that book; those interested in a more formal and substantial discussion of the controversies and history surrounding women's ordination may wish to consult chapter 4 of *New Cath-olic Women*.

The headnotes introducing the essays are meant to situate them in the context of my professional life and within my own personal struggle to find a place for myself as a feminist within my religious tradition. Each essay marks an opportunity for me to understand a particular issue within the general framework of women's spiritual-ity, but I would not be able to address anyone had I not had to confront the ambiguities of my own identity transformation and the dislocations of my own spiritual quest.

In the 1970s I listened, for the most part, to women who re-mained active within the Catholic church while voicing some sig-nificant criticism of its structures and practices. As that decade wore on, I found myself talking with women whose decisions to leave the "patriarchal church" behind became the occasion of sorrow, terror, exhilaration, and solidarity. By the early 1980s, I was immersed in the historical project of trying to chronicle the intersection of the women's movement with the American Catholic church.

New Catholic Women, written in 1985, tended to concentrate on women in the large middle section of an ideological bell curve. In the past few years, I have become more interested in women on the extremes of that curve. My essay on Goddess religion is an attempt to understand the need some women have had to leave their churches or synagogues in order to participate in the revival of an ancient (or the creation of a new) religion devoted to the Goddess. At present, I am engaged in a project that will help me to understand women on the right-wing margins of the American Catholic church, women whose religious lives are rooted in devotion to the Virgin Mary and to a highly traditional understanding of the place of women in church and family.

Throughout this book, it will be obvious that I continue to return to certain wellsprings of the Catholic tradition even when I am trying to understand something radically new. I doubt that autobiography can fully explain this tendency of mine, but I grew up in the tradi-tional Catholicism of the 1940s and 1950s and was drawn to stories about transformative journeys. The spiritual language of my youth was that of quest; the images were often drawn from a romantically remembered medieval tradition passed on to me by my teachers. My love for Teresa of Avila and John of the Cross comes from my mother, I think, though I do not remember her suggesting them so much as reading and rereading them herself. When my mother died this past summer, she had just finished rereading *The Odyssey* and was looking once more at Teresa's *The Way of Perfection*, so perhaps I come to these texts with a certain natural predisposition toward them.

Whatever problem of dislocation I find myself wrestling with, I seem always to return to the mainstays of my spiritual support system: I fell in love with Dante in college and I look to him because his poetry affirms the value of images and asks me to pay attention to the events and drama of this world; I read Teresa of Avila because her mystical journey is grounded in an understanding of herself in relation to a deity at once beyond this world and profoundly present in her own soul. Dante and Teresa feed my yearning for adventure and discovery in spiritual terms: they both wrestle with the great questions—dependence/independence, intimacy/distance, unity/diversity—that mark everyday human life and describe the essence of spirituality.

SPRINGS *of*
WATER *in a*
DRY LAND

AT HOME IN HER OWN HOUSE

A Search for God in Feminist Experience

When I confronted the problem of women in the church for the *Future of American Catholicism* conference in Washington, D.C., in 1988, I was overwhelmed by women's sense of dislocation. I had spent many years talking with Catholic women who simply felt that they had no place to go. Like me, many grew up in the Catholic church before the Second Vatican Council and had been nourished by its traditions and sacraments, oblivious to sexist language, patriarchal preference, and other painful discoveries of the feminist movement in the churches. In trying to place women in the postconciliar church, as I was asked to do in Washington, I created the four stories I used to introduce this book. I wanted to reflect on the range of dislocation women have felt as they attempt to understand themselves as faithful Catholics and convinced feminists.

But in writing this essay, I realized that I was no longer content to describe the pain and anguish that marked those four stories. At the same time, I was not sanguine about finding realistic alternatives. The intellectual problem I faced writing this essay was, at the same time, a profoundly personal one: I wanted to find a way to imagine constructive movement toward a viable spirituality in the context of the variety of spiritual choices women have been making for themselves for the past several years. At least the second part of my task was relatively easy: I could explain why many women eagerly identified themselves as feminists, given the experience of women in the fifties, and could use it to delineate some of the various ways feminist women in the Catholic church have attempted to live with what seems to be an oxymoronic identity.

I hoped that the first part of my goal would somehow "come to me" once I had set the contextual stage. I do not know why I thought there was something magical in historical context. I suppose it indicates how frustrated I felt: I had been wrestling with questions of feminist spirituality for fifteen years and still had no grand ideas about how one might resolve the ambiguities involved in trying to maintain an identity that was both Catholic and feminist.

I tried to think about the problem in purely personal terms: how could I make sense of the Catholic tradition for myself *in a way that supported my feminism?* The result of that line of thinking was a deepening sense of frustration that forced me to spend more time with my own prayer life.

I began by sitting quietly with Teresa of Avila. When, reading through her autobiography, I came to the passage with which I begin this essay, I knew I had found what I was looking for. Teresa seems to me to have been "at home in her own house" precisely to the extent that she listened to God's voice within her, that is to say, to the extent that she trusted her own experience. I do not mean to suggest that Teresa was a feminist. We are not served by anachronistic identifications, and Teresa would likely be stunned and distressed by the agenda of the modern feminist movement and by the hostility and anguish one meets there. At the same time, the power of her own self-acceptance in a historical situation that demanded self-abnegation is astonishing and gave me something I found useful both personally and in writing this essay.

A mystic, someone once said, is simply a person who takes a long loving look at reality. A more homey way to put it might be to say that spirituality requires that we do what needs to be done without worrying too much if our efforts are going to result in ultimate changes in the system. The "solution," if indeed that is the right word, is rooted for me in those parts of the tradition that patriarchy cannot control, in my own responses to the "moments, incidents, and choices" in my life as I move around in the world. I discovered my closing quotation from Evelyn Underhill quite by accident. It reminds me that there is an element of mystery in all this possibility and that "this vast work of transformation" is what needs to be done.

Mystical language from contemplative people, however much it soothes my own troubled spirit, must not lead to passivity and a reluctance to confront the problems that surround us. It is useful because it can free us from the need to expect major changes or to measure our success by someone else's standards. When push comes to shove, we have to trust one another as Catholics and as feminists. All of us, moving around or firmly rooted upon the spectrum I describe in this essay, make choices that sometimes have agonizing results. To confront those moments on a daily basis and not be defeated by them requires us to be "at home in our own house."

Once, while at prayer with her sisters, Teresa of Avila was drawn into a profound religious vision in which she perceived her soul as a mirror, brightly polished and totally clear. In the center was Christ, permeating every part of her soul so that she was able to see him clearly. What makes this extraordinary experience even more remarkable, however, is what Teresa saw when she looked upon her beloved: "This mirror also—I don't know how to explain it—was completely engraved upon the Lord Himself."[1] In other words, she looked into herself and saw Christ, then looked into Christ and saw herself, a wise woman, engraved upon the divine object of her desire. This mutual imprinting is a theme not foreign to mystical experience, but perhaps not always exploited for its full value. Clearly Teresa had achieved the state of mutual indwelling that marks the apogee of self-*donation*. Less obvious, perhaps, is the radical self-*possession* of her statement. Constance Fitzgerald says that "Teresa's heart had found its dwelling place. Yet she herself was a dwelling place. She was at home in her own house."[2]

This sixteenth-century Spanish Carmelite was "at home" just as far as she was willing to trust her own experience to redefine the central symbol of her religious life. To a very great extent, Teresa reconstructed God. She had the courage to imagine God as a lover interested in her strength rather than in her weakness. Had she followed the religious streams of her time and place, she would have relinquished her own vision in favor of those who understood God to be more concerned with domination than with equality.[3] Had she allowed herself to be carried along by the spiritual currents of late medieval Spain rather than by God's affirmation of her own judgment, she would have had to believe that God's will is usually at odds with our own desires rather than in tune with them. Teresa's experience empowered her and helped her to claim her own wisdom. If her early writings are sometimes marred by denigration of herself as a woman, "her later writings stand as a clear and forceful defense of women's wisdom."[4]

Teresa could not have succeeded in the daily excitement and frustration of a major religious reformation had she been a fearful, subservient woman. To her way of understanding, God needed her to be strong enough to withstand patriarchal criticism and capable enough to imagine fruitful alternatives to the stagnating models of religious life she found around her. The ground for these heroic virtues was her own experience as one deeply related to and trusted by God. Her connectedness with a God imagined in terms of intimacy and mutual support gave her the courage to reach beyond the God of the "Fathers." Had she not trusted her own experience, she might never have been at home in her own house.

The Experience of Homelessness

In sharp contrast with Teresa's confidence about her place in God's scheme of things, I often find myself describing my own situation as one of spiritual homelessness. However profoundly I am indebted to the insights of feminism to support a reliance on my own experience, and however clearly I am able to relate my personal struggles to the religious reality of a spiritual quest, I am nonetheless anxious about the outcome. Like many women who have rejected patriarchal religion, I am as yet without a real alternative. My own experience— perhaps yours as well—is marked by a sense of loss I can articulate but find hard to bear.

Were I to continue my story in Carmelite terms, I could describe the impasse many women now experience as a modern "dark night of the soul."[5] As satisfying as such an interpretation might be for the mystically inclined, however, I do not believe it is the best pathway out of a modern spiritual quandary. I am caught, as I believe many are, in a tangle of unavoidable suffering. How we got here bears some review. How we might escape requires our collective patience, imagination, and action.

Below, I examine feminism in the lives of American women and in the lives of women in the Roman Catholic church. Both contexts have had an aura of embattlement and challenge about them because in both American culture and in the American Catholic church, those to whom women complained tended to marginalize their case. When feminism became a household word in the late sixties, it was connected with trivializing stereotypes: feminists were "women's libbers," who made public spectacles of themselves by burning bras and whose needs for individual advancement led to an angry rejection of motherhood, child rearing, and femininity itself. When feminists came to the attention of the American Catholic hierarchy in the seventies, most bishops chose to label them as radicals and to warn the faithful against their aberrations. In spite of rigorous opposition, however, women have continued to press their case and have resisted efforts to keep them locked away in suburbia or in the sacristy.

THE FIFTIES

In order to contextualize the kinds of options available to women in the church, we should take some time to remember that the twentieth-century women's movement began *not* in the church, but in a specific moment in American cultural history, the fifties. Before moving to ecclesial territory, we need to understand women's lives in the fifties, the decade that vilified female independence by insisting on what Betty Friedan called "the feminine mystique."[6] Television programs like "Dick van Dyke," "Father Knows Best," "Ozzie and Harriet," and "Leave It to Beaver" celebrated a nuclear family headed by a wise father ruling benevolently over his compliant partner and their charming children. Although this picture attempted to describe only the lives of white middle-class women, it had "a breathtaking power to induce conformity."[7] The American Dream was built upon the idea that anatomy was destiny and that women should devote themselves to and find total satisfaction in marriage and motherhood.

The power of Friedan's book—which was published just as the Second Vatican Council opened in Rome—lay in its ability to shed light on the shadow side of the American Dream. Friedan found that "the very power of the feminine mystique to limit women's aspirations and choices also created a vast underground of seething discontent."[8] The cheerful theme songs of family sitcoms were the background music for women's private nightmares.

Fifties housewives, Friedan discovered, "quietly endured profound despair, interminable boredom and unbearable isolation. Working women, whose numbers doubled during the fifties, quietly suffered sexual discrimination and harassment on their jobs. Daughters, sensing the bitterness and disappointment of their mothers, entered the new decade mapping escape routes."[9] The mothers and daughters of the fifties became the feminists of the sixties, launching a revolution whose agenda was to exorcise the nightmare for themselves and for the nation.

Perceiving themselves as warriors against the spirit of the fifties, feminists engaged in political action and bellicose rhetoric. Whereas politically minded older women (the mothers) founded the National Organization for Women to take up a liberal program for the rights of women, the more radical, younger women (the disgruntled daughters) questioned everything and angrily denounced men, marriage, and motherhood. Ruth Rosen has noted that the rage of some women in the early stages of the feminist movement made it impossible for them to work constructively. "Extreme moralism, unwillingness to tolerate difference, inability to appreciate the sexual and economic fear of dependent women, failure to comprehend the importance of racial and class divisions and ambivalence toward authority all helped undermine the women's movement's ability to speak compellingly to the majority of American women on all but a few issues."[10]

American feminists have struggled for a generation to move beyond the fear and anger of the early years. The simple-minded version of the American Dream has been replaced in women's lives by the realities of a changing, complicated world. However much one may yearn for a placid life, few of us would trade our struggle for a life with Kitten, Bud, and Princess in a realm where "father knows best." The women's movement is a fact of our present lives that has challenged us to find creative alternatives in our own small spheres even as it has drawn us into a nexus of complex international problems and connected us with the urgency of planetary survival.[11]

FEMINISM AND THE BISHOPS

As we ponder the problems we face as women searching for spiritual alternatives to the "faith of our fathers," it is useful to remember the political context of feminism. What we find in the Roman Catholic church is not dissimilar to what I have just described. In 1990, the American Catholic bishops, in the second draft of their pastoral letter on women in the church, described feminism as something to be avoided. The bishops, in one sweeping paragraph, "caution Catholic women not to advocate, as some radical feminist groups do, such aberrations as goddess worship, witchcraft, liberation from conformity to the sexual morality taught by the church or acceptance of abortion as a legitimate choice for women under pressure."[12] If you have thought about or practiced artificial birth control, if you believe that abortion should be *discussed* in terms of women's moral agency, if you see reasons to change God-language in your prayer lives, or believe that such language is metaphorical and therefore capable of change, if you believe women ought to be ordained to the priesthood or that celibacy ought to be optional, if you think that little girls can be acolytes as well as little boys, you are in good company. Unfortunately, you are also seen as a danger to those women whom the bishops regard as "loyal Catholic women."

The second draft of the pastoral letter was yet another eviction notice served on Catholic feminists by ecclesiastical authorities. It should not be surprising that it called forth an enraged response. In an open letter to the American Catholic hierarchy signed by feminist and liberal groups within the church, Rosemary Ruether accused the bishops of trying to seduce women into helping them rescue their patriarchal ecclesial system while conceding nothing essential to that system:

> You want us to throw our energies into, not only sweeping the floors, washing the linens, baking the cookies, serving the coffee, arranging the flowers, but also now doing the pastoral counseling, organizing the catechetics, playing the music, even leading the prayers, above all, raising the money, for a celibate male, clerical, patriarchal church which is disintegrating at its center precisely because of the celibate male, clerical patriarchal assumptions to which you cling so desperately. . . .
>
> We will not raise one cent for your patriarchal church. We will not lift one finger to rescue your patriarchal system. We will not bend one knee to worship the patriarchal idol that you blasphemously insist on calling "God." We are not fooled. We have heard the gospel of the authentic Jesus, the Christ; good news to the poor, release to the captives, the setting at liberty of those who are oppressed. We are raising money to promote the ministries of that authentic gospel. We are pouring our energies into serving that community of liberation, where we find our real sisters and brothers of the Catholic household, and many other households as well. We are standing with arms raised in delight and celebration with that Holy Wisdom who truly created us and calls for the redemption of all of us, together with our suffering mother, the earth. This is the Redeemer that we love. This is the community that we serve.[13]

The tone of Ruether's response and the language she used no doubt alarm some women in the church much the way the angry rhetoric of early feminism frightened women in mainstream culture. But just as the rage of sixties feminism was a radical cry of pain that eventually opened new paths of dialogue and creative interaction with women of different classes, races, and nations, so it is possible that our anger can generate new models of spiritual and religious life. American Catholic women in the nineties constitute a complicated group, and we cannot begin to address what we might need until we have some idea of who we are.

AMERICAN CATHOLIC WOMEN

Whether in the traditions of the church or the draft of the bishops' pastoral letter, women are still defined by Catholicism essentially in terms of motherhood. While fatherhood is an option men may choose as they explore ways to define themselves as persons, motherhood is seen as a necessary component of female nature. One does not have to make a case against motherhood to notice that there is something disjointed about the absolute coupling of motherhood with women's identity. It is as if, in these days of cable television reruns, the American bishops are still watching "Father Knows Best" as a popular account of the proper roles for and values of women.

There are of course women in the culture and in the church who would agree with that description of their natures and their lives. Many of them are located on the right wings of the political and ecclesiastical spectrum, where they fear feminism as a danger to the nuclear family and to the continued health of the church. I think we must, where we can, listen to antifeminist women in the Catholic church and attempt to see, in their own faithfulness to the tradition, a solution that works for them in ways we might not fully appreciate. I will focus here, however, on those of us who are uneasy about the bishops' letter, neither fully at home in the present institution nor able to abandon it.

When I look around in the Roman Catholic church, I see those women I wrote about in *New Catholic Women*.[14] Just as American culture is no longer identifiable in terms of the fifties nuclear family, neither is the church made up primarily of wives and mothers content to assume a complementary role to their husbands. To be sure, the majority of women in the church are married with children. That majority is not as overwhelming today as it was, but it is still considerable. Women in the contemporary church have an extraordinarily complicated range of life styles matched by a daunting set of needs.

American Catholics are more diverse today than at any other time in their history. If American Catholic women ever were adequately described in terms of the stereotype of the American Dream, they are no longer so neatly categorized. The number of married women with large families who send their children to Catholic schools while they pour their energies into homemaking, child rearing, and volunteer parish work is dwindling rapidly. Women still choose marriage as a primary option, but very few have the economic security to stay home, and very few of them have large families. The future of the Catholic school system is not at all clear at this point, nor can anyone feel secure about the future of the traditional parish.

More to the point, the American Catholic church contains vast numbers of women whose needs are not being met. Many of these women are vocal about their discomfort. Some suffer in silence. Today the American Catholic church has within it various groups of nuns with new ideas and new vocations to political and social activism. Many of them are under pressure to conform to a pattern of religious life they no longer find spiritually sustaining. In our church, we find single mothers struggling to survive in a culture that does little to alleviate their double burden. Given the statistical averages for divorce in this country, the church now has a significant number of women who are single for the first time, or who have remarried and now must deal with the exigencies of creating alternative family situations. Although there may be generous "pastoral solutions" to some of their problems in some situations, divorced or remarried Catholics who try to remain "in the church" generally do so with substantial anguish. Similarly, lesbians searching for partners, or involved in committed relationships, must withstand the general hostility of Catholicism to any idea that homosexual unions can be occasions for graceful growth in the spirit. Women in marriages of convenience or in abusive situations often get little or no sympathy or support from their pastors, and they often find a more congenial community in women's groups or shelters. Some of the single women who make up the Catholic church live alone wondering how, exactly, the church values them aside from their ability to contribute their services to its efficient functioning. Other single women are members of communities, like the Grail, committed to international feminism and to a new vision grounded in but not limited by traditional Catholicism.

How can one attempt to imagine the spiritual needs of such a diverse group? Some would be happy in the institutional church if only they could be ordained or have their "irregular" partnership arrangements—remarriage after divorce or homosexual union—blessed by the local priest. Others, taking up the slogans of Vatican II, refuse to let themselves be defined by ecclesiastical authorities even as they engage in practices and are supported by beliefs that the institutional church finds odious. Some look forward to a church without a clerical base where the Eucharist can be celebrated by members of the local community in faithfulness to the commands of Jesus, while others envision an eclectic liturgy that builds on the Catholic tradition even as it widens its parameters beyond any traditional boundaries. Some have found refuge in what we used to call "underground" or "floating" parishes, and others call themselves "recovering Catholics," unable to live with Catholicism and unable, somehow, to live without it. Do these choices represent an impossible situation for Catholic feminists, or might we think about them from a different perspective?

God Imagined in Old and New Ways

Aware of the dangers of generalizing from my own experience, I am nevertheless going to hazard a common denominator of discontent for Catholic feminists. The problem for many women in the church is patriarchal Catholicism, and the most fundamental issue within that system is the symbol of God. Patriarchal Catholicism worships a limited God and demands that women fit into a spiritual system where we cannot, by definition, find a place for ourselves. I am not making a case against the deity. Far from it. I believe that many women in the church are homeless because we attempt to worship a Being whose attributes do not resonate with our experience. We suffer because we try to fit our spiritual aspirations into a space that is more restrictive and less magnificent than we know to be true.

The idea that our language about or understanding of God is wrong or inadequate is hardly new. Feminists who have abandoned religion altogether have done so because the central symbol of Western religious life is described in male terms and seems to operate primarily in patterns of domination and submission. Feminists who have left traditional Judaism and Christianity in an attempt to find spiritual solace in "the Goddess" have done so precisely because "God is a symbol which may have outlived its usefulness as an exclusive mediator between humans and the ultimate reality that grounds and sustains their lives."[15] Those feminist theologians who have remained attached to their religious traditions have often been able to do so because they are able to reimagine the traditional God in more satisfying terms. Sallie McFague, for example, begins her reconstruction of the doctrine of the Trinity by asking "whether the Judeo-Christian tradition's triumphalist imagery for the relationship between God and the world is helpful or harmful."[16]

When I talk about a "limited God," therefore, I am arguing that our ways of explaining divinity have been lopsided in favor of one particular symbolic formation. The predominant features of the God we find in traditional Catholicism and conservative Protestantism are essentially patriarchal. *He* exists in isolation, all-knowing and all-powerful, presiding over a world ordered by His will. His attributes and interests are conspicuously and stereotypically masculine, and like the Victorian father, He is best approached through intermediaries. He functions necessarily as a judge, sometimes harsh but always fair. Even in cases of innocent suffering, He is never culpable. He masters the chaos of the universe and expects men to master their passions and to control their women and their children. He is in control, a metaphysical essence who is above the suffering that marks creaturely life. He apparently appreciates strong, willful men and compliant, obedient women. One submits to Him, begs His favor, and hopes never to offend His divine will.

Although this picture of God has for many years been the predominant one, it is not the only one available in the Christian tradition. God as disclosed in the Bible is not simply a patriarch whose name and existence underwrite hierarchical structures and male domination of women. One can find biblical images of God as compassionate, nurturing, suffering, and longing for union with humankind. In the Catholic tradition and in the mystical literature, one can find

a God with quite a different set of characteristics, a lover able to relate
to human beings in terms of mutuality and longing.

Saint Augustine (354–430), for example, may be remembered as
a brilliant fifth-century philosopher with gifts of abstract reasoning,
but a great part of his charm rests in his "romantic" search for union
with the kind of cosmic love God represented to him. Augustine was
willing to relinquish an extraordinarily promising career in order to
pursue the desire of his restless heart.[17] His *Confessions* still compel
attention because they disclose this relentless longing more clearly
than they explain the great pursuits of his mind. Like other lovers,
Augustine trusted his experience. His *Confessions* reveal the passionate longing for limitless experience that bespeaks a God more tender
than a list of patriarchal attributes permits us to imagine.

Dante Alighieri (1265–1321), the great medieval poet, also
trusted his heart. In *The Divine Comedy*, he recapitulates the cosmic
drama of salvation in terms of romantic love. The object of that love
is a young woman, Beatrice, but it is also, in some mysterious way,
God. Seeing Beatrice, he sees divinity, and having known God
through the experience of falling in love, he is moved to venture
through hell and purgatory in search of another vision of her. In the
last cantos of "Purgatory," when Dante finally meets his beloved
Beatrice on the threshold of heaven, she is costumed as—in some
miraculous way she *is*—the Blessed Sacrament, worthy of earthly
and heavenly adoration. At the same time she is, Dante tells us, more
formidable than an angry mother is to a disobedient son, able to
break his heart and chastise his spirit.

I have mentioned these two great male figures of the Roman Catholic tradition to suggest that God disclosed in the relationship of
lover to beloved is not specific to the female religious imagination.
Teresa of Avila, far removed in time and place from Augustine and
Dante, had a similar experience. What distinguishes her from them
is her sex. Augustine was a bishop, an authority figure whose interpretations of Catholic doctrine gave him a place of reverence in the
early church. Dante was a renowned poet, the father of the Italian
language, who overcame personal disgrace to become one of the
world's great luminaries. Teresa had no title, no power, no authority.

On the contrary, her words were edited and censored by male religious authorities. Her vision of God and her ideas for a renewed religious life placed her under constant suspicion. She was forced to trust in herself and in her experience without benefit of approval in her lifetime.

Catholic women who struggle with their feminism in the context of their religious tradition have come to a moment where we must do as Teresa did in much the same way, though we are luckier than Teresa in having a supportive community of women with whom to share the struggle. Although we too may be accused of delusion, arrogance, and heresy by patriarchal authorities, we do not have to labor under the paralyzing burden of fear induced by the Inquisition. We can, like Teresa, come to understand that God needs strong, capable women to carry humanity further along the pathways of divine love and mutual interaction, and we are not limited in our reading by an Index of Forbidden Books. Like Teresa we must be confident enough to be fearless, and ardent enough to be relentless.

Having set the stage for a reconceptualization of spirituality, what might we propose as its drama? If the patriarchal God is inadequate, is "the Goddess" any more compelling? Is the Buddha? Can we nourish ourselves in the springs of the mystical tradition if we are not mystics? Can we find a home in the spiritual territory of liberation theology? Is there a warrant for preferring the personality of the process God? Can we find what we need within the Catholic tradition? These are some of the questions with which we must come to terms. I believe we must also be prepared for new visions of a truly catholic spirituality, which must be informed by our struggles within the institutional church and by the vexing realities of our world.

Feminist interpreters of religion tend to separate into five more or less distinct groups along a spectrum that runs from satisfaction with the status quo to angry rejection of the tradition. For Catholic women responding to the bewildering interactions of Catholicism and feminism, these five groupings are like major cities on a road map. They are written in large type to get our attention, but they are not the only places one can visit and surely not the only places worthy of attention. At the same time, I believe these five responses to the women's movement on the part of Catholic women make a fascinating narrative of spiritual growth and development within the groups themselves and in relation to one another.

TRADITIONALISTS

The first and most conservative response to feminism is staying put. At the right extreme, one finds a group made up of women who are still nourished spiritually by Catholicism as it is, or as it was before the Second Vatican Council. A Catholic woman troubled or angered by the questions raised by feminists can grasp the tradition firmly, seeing her complementary role as something essentially positive, valorizing female saints, and delighting in the strength of some of the many remarkable women in the history of Catholicism. For many such women, Mary the mother of God is both a role model and a source of comfort and strength.

These women may be convinced antifeminists or may simply be uninterested in the criticisms of the women's movement. They may have been drawn to some of the early discussions raised by feminists, but finally are unable to attempt an alternative formulation of their faith. In other words, those women who claim to be satisfied with Catholicism as it is may well be happy in the patriarchal church. But if they are unhappy, they are nonetheless unwilling to relinquish their Catholic heritage.

Traditional Catholic women who fit into this category may be active in prolife movements, finding in that work a special kind of Catholic identity which corresponds with the directives of the hierarchy and the inclinations of their own hearts. They may be members of religious orders that have not warmed to all the changes in religious life over the past twenty-five years. They find a satisfactory spiritual life along the lines specified centuries ago in the writings of the great medieval theologians and saints.

In the wider world of American Christianity, many conservative Christian women—Evangelicals, Pentecostals, and Mormons, for example—fit this description. They believe that the biblical text is an eternal truth, always valid, and generally good. Since it is the Word of God, it may not be rejected. The challenge to humans is to conform to this ancient expression of divine authority. Traditionalists have developed sophisticated interpretive perspectives to defend their position, usually placing the blame for troublesome interpretations at the feet of the interpreter.

GODDESS FEMINISTS

On the left wing of the spectrum, we find those feminists who have rejected traditional religion without relinquishing their belief that a religious dimension is an important part of human experience. Some women in this radical position are attracted to the meditative practices of Zen Buddhism. Others have poured their religious energy into a search for "the Goddess." Both alternatives require conversion to a new religion and to a new kind of spirituality.

The Roman Catholic church has recently issued a document warning Catholics against a too friendly appropriation of Buddhist or Hindu practices. I myself cannot speak at any length about such influences, but it is perhaps enough to know that men like Thomas Merton and Bede Griffiths have found sustenance and dialogue partners in Eastern religions. Many Catholics continue to be interested in these great traditions. Whether they are "good for women" is not clear to me, especially as one can find texts attributed to the Buddha that are extremely disdainful of women.

Compared with secular feminists who find *any* religious dimension evidence of a delusional or neurotic personality, Goddess feminists appear to be relatively conservative. Compared with feminists who still cling in some way to traditional religion, however, Goddess feminists appear to be generating a new vision of the future based on incomplete or misleading historical information. Those who worship some form of the Goddess and who practice witchcraft as a revival of an ancient woman-centered religion claim to reach back over six millennia of patriarchal religion to a far older faith, though the historical evidence for this older faith remains elusive.[18] Still, Goddess feminists and traditional religionists share a general respect for religion in human life, and they both understand the need for community and long for some ritual reenactments of a central religious vision.

Neopaganism rests on a utopian rather than a historical vision. Those at this point on the spectrum reject the ancient texts, finding them inexorably patriarchal and harmful for women. Because they are able to conclude that the Bible is the "word of man" rather than a divinely inspired text, they are not usually textbound. What causes some women to move toward neopaganism and others to cling to tradition? Perhaps the choice between traditionalism and neopaganism rests more on religious autobiography than it does on rational argument. Some people are more hurt by their traditions than others are by the same traditions; some are more nourished because they have explored options that others have not.

REVISIONISTS

Revisionists attempt to occupy an encompassing position along the spectrum that embraces both tradition and change. Revisionary feminists attempt to reread traditional texts and reinterpret traditional practices in ways that uncover the often hidden but nonetheless powerful presence of women. Revisionists continue to be active within the Roman Catholic church and faithful to its traditions. They work from within the institution, trying to make the language of the liturgy sex-inclusive and seeing to it that both men and women are active in various ministries.

A revisionary feminist may be a member of the Women's Ordination Conference, perhaps even feeling herself called to active ministry in the priesthood. She sees that some structural changes may have to occur within the church, but she also imagines that feminists might have a major impact on the institution as it is presently embodied so long as lines of dialogue are kept open.

Although the revisionary position is initially exhilarating, many women find it ultimately disappointing. In the beginning, it is a great boost to the spirit to rediscover powerful women in the tradition, to find women who held ecclesiastical office, to expose the patriarchal assumptions of canon law, or to suggest, as I have done, that Mary might function as an icon of the women's movement. Finally, however, revisionary reading occurs within the confines of a tradition that grows increasingly intractable on women's issues.

A revisionary feminist who may no longer believe it possible to revise biblical texts or liturgical celebrations may mix Sunday mass with occasional feminist liturgies and think that a revisionary reading of the text ought to include extracanonical sources. At the theological level, revisionary feminists might turn to process thought, which understands God in terms of immanence and vulnerability as well as in the more traditional language of transcendence and power. Process theology (as we shall see) is an imperfect but nevertheless intriguing system which is attractive to feminists partly because it seems to verify their religious experience.

MYSTICS

The point between the middle ground (revisionism) and the right end of the spectrum (traditionalism) is occupied by the mystics, those who find a satisfying spiritual life through contemplation. Mystics have sometimes used language that feminists find retrograde. The glorification of the "eternal feminine," for example, however much it might appear to exalt women and celebrate female nature, tends to imprison real women on a cosmic pedestal. The valorization of "femininity" as found in some nineteenth-century spiritual writers segregates women by defining female nature as different from male nature. Women, in this view, are naturally generous, life-giving, spiritually minded, and nurturing.

Interestingly, while this general line of thought appeals to conservative women, it also forms part of the foundation for a radical feminist Goddess religion. From whatever direction one approaches this point, however, the underlying problems appear to be the same. Those who affirm a separate, higher natural status for women see that as human beings men and women are essentially different. In this dual-nature anthropology, men and women are destined for different roles in life. Since the feminist movement in the past two centuries has adamantly denied separate roles and natures, it is bewildering to find contemporary radical feminists reaffirming women's differences. Radical feminists find those two natures at war with one another and label males as inherently necrophilic.[19] Conservative women, on the other hand, find those two natures complementary to one another and tend to discuss union in terms of the needs men and women have for one another in order to form a complete humanity.

Another dimension of mysticism rejects the glorification of the female found in the devotees of the "eternal feminine" and prefers instead to follow the symbolic/erotic language of the mystical tradition. This path surely appealed to Teresa of Avila and liberated her from the constraints of the church she encountered. Similarly, the language of the "dark night of the soul" is for many a fruitful way of overcoming present agonies and trusting in a future dawn. Mysticism has a worldwide appeal because it draws one into a personal, intimate relationship with the deity. As a feminist spiritual option, however, it is problematic, an odd vocation in the modern world. J. D. Salinger's character, Teddy, the mystical religious genius in a short story named for him, tells a young man that "it's very hard to meditate and live a spiritual life in America. People think you are a freak if you try to."[20] I cannot imagine someone leading a mystical life outside of a monastery or some self-created space away from the distractions of the world. If that is the case, then the mystical option, albeit personally satisfying, is not suited to an active life in the world. Mysticism is more tuned to individual spiritual growth than it is responsive to the political questions of the feminist movement. Still, the very nature of mysticism reminds us that we must never underestimate its power to transform consciousness beyond the walls of its enclosures.

LIBERATIONISTS

The point between the middle ground (revisionists) and the left extreme (neopaganism) is occupied by the liberationists, those who find God revealed most clearly in the lives of the poor and whose spirituality is marked by political activism. Their inspiration comes from various third world experiments associated with liberation theology, which builds upon a biblical base reinterpreted so that human liberation contains and discloses the meaning of salvation. Here God is found among the marginalized and the dispossessed. As a critical reflection on a top-down model of revelation, liberation theology appeals to those who find God's most authentic self-disclosure in various struggles for freedom. It thus has a natural connection with feminism and binds feminists and others to radical commitment to anyone still imprisoned by jailers, patriarchs, economic exploiters, military leaders, or any system of determined repression. At the same time, seeing that the planet itself is struggling under various kinds of oppression, adherents tend to be drawn into the environmental movement as well.

Those feminists who need to go beyond revisionism but are unable to accept fully the presuppositions and goals of neopaganism are often attracted to some form of liberationism. The women's movement within the Roman Catholic church is often explained in terms of liberation theology, an attractive option for those who read biblical texts in terms of divine initiatives of redemption. For them the exodus story in the Bible is a tale of freedom from captivity and oppression. It becomes a paradigm for God's intentions in the world today.

However appealing liberation theology is to feminist sensibilities, and however pertinent to feminist and other struggles, there are questions that should be asked about it. I wonder first of all about the third world base of liberation theology. Can a theological position built upon communities in situations of massive political and economic distress make a fruitful transition to a first world culture? In what ways can we use the impetus of liberation theology in our own lives if those lives are fairly comfortable and middle class? Must we relinquish our worldly goods? If we do not, is there something false in our position? If the God of liberation theology is revealed most clearly in the lives of the poor and calls for us to *live with* the poor in order to experience a transformed consciousness, what does that mean for our lives now? As I consider these questions, I am haunted by the character in T. S. Eliot's play *The Cocktail Party* whose longing for God impels her to a missionary vocation in Africa, where she is savagely martyred by being tied to an anthill and eaten alive. Closer to home, perhaps, was the news of the four American women killed in El Salvador in 1981 and the thousands who have risked or given their lives in the tortured political contexts of Latin America. Does the liberationist God require such heroic sacrifice?

Conclusion

None of the above positions is pure. Each of them tends to overlap somewhat with the position closest to it on the spectrum. Similarly, few Catholic women fit securely and snugly into one single spot. Spirituality is dynamic, and growth can be experienced in both directions. Some women who have explored the possibilities of feminism have moved steadily to the left, while others have maintained a traditional position and grown spiritually deeper because of it. All have been touched in different ways by the Second Vatican Council, by the women's movement, and by the ineffable movement of the Spirit in their lives. All have different and profoundly rich religious autobiographies that call them to be more daring or compel them to be more cautious in their religious lives. The challenge for us all is to listen carefully to as many voices as we can. Those on the extremes may be unable to hear one another, while those in the middle may be blessed or cursed with an ability to hear too many women talking at one time.

How does one choose among them? *Must* we choose among them? Is it possible to find a satisfying spirituality by concentrating on aspects of each position? I do not know. My own efforts to find an eclectic alternative have not been very satisfying. Still, there is something to be said for the search itself. Like many Catholic women I have met, I long for something I cannot name and desire a community of belief and celebration I cannot yet describe.

In the end I find myself falling back on the kind of language Catholicism has always used to describe spirituality. The language of the spiritual *quest* for transformation coupled with an expanded notion of vocation. The feminist religious vocation requires the everyday heroism of small things. In other words, we must do what we can in the context in which we live. Evelyn Underhill says it quite beautifully: "Our whole life is to be poised on a certain glad expectancy of God, taking each moment, incident, choice, and opportunity as material placed in our hands by the Creator, whose whole intricate and mysterious process moves toward the triumph of charity and who has given each living spirit a tiny part in this vast network of transformation."[21]

I believe, finally, that we will get to where we are going by trusting our experience, by believing that our deepest desires are, in truth, God's desires for us. Christianity is not complete as it is. The churches need our voices, those that complain and those that comply. The divine being has not been fully disclosed in the language and practice of patriarchy. If we abandon the struggle, we might as well admit that the patriarchal articulation of God is the only one possible. That would be deeply tragic. God has been imprisoned by patriarchy just as we have. If, like Teresa, we can look into our souls and see a mirror reflecting the divine presence to us by showing how deeply we, ourselves, are engraved on the spirit of Wisdom, then we can be nurtured by her strength and follow her example. We can, in other words, do what needs to be done however strange, arrogant, heretical, or peculiar it may look to those whose religious visions of the future are limited by the confining categories of the past.

IN SEARCH OF THE GRAIL

An Experiment in

Community

I*f, as I said earlier, spirituality requires that we do what needs to be done without worrying too much about results, then it is important to find real places in the world where that outlook prevails. The Grail movement, headquartered on nearly two hundred acres of rolling Ohio farmland, is a community experiment that embodies that freedom of spirit. Furthermore, it is a good case study of a group of decidedly feminist women who are rooted in Catholic faith and liturgical celebration but open to a wide range of religious expression. This essay was originally written in 1990 to celebrate the fiftieth anniversary of the Grail in the United States.*

The Grail, an international women's collective, was founded in Holland in 1929 to give Catholic women an alternative to marriage and family. It was meant to serve a practical need by way of religious idealism, or in the language of the times, "to employ surplus women in the service of the church." We need to recall the aftermath of World War I: there were so many more women than men in Europe that marriage was not taken for granted by nearly all women as it had been, and there was much work to be done. Jacques van Ginneken (1877–1945), the Jesuit founder of the Grail, looked upon the many single women in Holland as a tremendous resource for the conversion of the world, a transformation he spoke of in terms of "the feminine" as much as in the language of Catholicism. "The ladies of the Grail," as he called them, would bring the domesticating and healing power of "the feminine" to a world nearly destroyed by bellicose masculinity.

Since the Grail was established in the United States in the 1940s, "the ladies of the Grail" have undergone some profound changes. In the early years, the Grail community—a group of single Catholic women living together without vows, but with a clear sense of mission—was a traditional movement with innovative ideas. In those days, the language and direction of the movement were not feminist in any modern understanding of the word. Yet since the Grail sought to empower women to make a difference in the world, it should not be surprising that the movement is now consciously feminist or that many members of the group believe that it has always been so.

I knew about the Grail throughout my childhood because the first American member of the movement had been my mother's roommate during her freshman year in college. When, a generation later, some of my own college professors tried to convince me that there were only two states of life appropriate for Catholic women—marriage or religious life—I used to cite the Grail as a counterexample. I had no personal interest in the movement, but the very existence of a group of single women named with the language of spiritual quest helped me to argue against what I perceived as an excessively narrow position about life's options. To tell the truth, I did not really see much real difference between joining the Grail and going to the convent. Neither choice attracted me. I remember reading an article about Grail women in Time *magazine in which their members were described as "nuns in mufti," a portrait that added nothing to their appeal for me. I went on with life after college without giving them another thought. I was astonished, therefore, as I began thinking about feminism and its place in the Catholic church, to find various Grail programs popping into my consciousness. The women in this movement were clearly not nuns; and just as clearly, they were forging new directions for women. By the time I wrote* New Catholic Women, *I had taken the opportunity to study their history and participate in some of their programs. I saw in the Grail, as I had seen in the lives of various communities of sisters, an ineluctable embrace of the women's movement that managed to affirm clear feminist principles without abandoning Catholicism.*

I began to wonder if members of communities were able to define themselves as Catholic feminists more easily than women "on the outside." Having spent more time now studying a few religious communities and the Grail movement,

*I see that their members struggle with the same problems as the rest of us.
Sometimes the community context is experienced as a great counterweight holding back more radical or forward-looking members, who see themselves as
having to contend not only with the traditions of the church, but with their
sister members. At the same time, the willingness of the collective to engage
in dialogue about difficult issues, to listen with sensitivity to the often painful
stories of its members, and to provide counsel and comfort in moments of
anguish, gives community members compelling reasons to be patient and to
continue the process of working through choices together.*

    *Grail members have had unique opportunities to be responsive to the needs
of our time and to adapt themselves to changing situations. Their movement
has proved both dedicated and flexible. The down-to-earth way Grail members lead their lives and imagine their future challenges my tendency to get
stuck in analysis and interpretation. I was pleased, therefore, to have this
chance to reflect on this group of (mostly) feminist (mostly) Catholic women.*

On a blustery March afternoon nearly two years before the United
States was to be fully engaged in the Second World War, two remarkable Dutch women embarked from a passenger liner in New
York harbor in distressed circumstances. Lydwine van Kersbergen
(b. 1904) and Joan Overboss (1910–69) had been on the last ship to
leave Holland: the Nazis invaded their country while they were en
route to America. Their money was worthless and their prospects
not altogether clear. No matter. Armed with a telegram of invitation
and a promise of some property from Chicago's auxiliary bishop,
Bernard Shiel, these two "ladies of the Grail" had their own ideas
about the future. On 19 May 1940, they moved to Doddrige Farm
in Libertyville, Illinois, to begin their part in an amazing chapter in
the history of American Catholicism. A half-century later, the
American branch of the Grail movement—headquartered near Cin-
cinnati, Ohio, since 1944—still enjoys the vision of remarkable
women and continues to have its own ideas about the future. It is
fitting in 1990, the fiftieth anniversary year, to recall some of the
history of the Grail movement in the United States and to look for

those signs that might tell us whether to expect new life or to prepare for a quiet retirement.

The question is perhaps best raised in the context of Alden Brown's *The Grail Movement and American Catholicism, 1940–1975*.[1] Brown's groundbreaking work traces the early history of the Grail movement in Holland but concentrates on its life in the United States as part of a larger Catholic revival. In the bulk of his book—the first eight of nine chapters—Brown makes a welcome contribution to American Catholic historiography: the Grail movement has been largely ignored by historians. I believe, however, that the last chapter, which attempts to make some judgments about the Grail based on events occurring since the Second Vatican Council, fails to address changing conditions in a way that allows for a fair evaluation.

Brown's interpretation is clearly rooted in the context of the resurgence of Catholic literary life that inspired Catholics from the mid-1930s to the mid-1960s. Dreams of a transformative Christian humanism based on Catholic ideas set goals for a generation. Sheed and Ward provided the books, French thinkers explained the new theology, and English spiritual writers nourished the inner lives of an impressive array of social activists. By including the Grail movement among those activists, Brown opens to view the connections between movements like the Grail, the National Catholic Rural Life Conference, the Catholic Family Movement, the Catholic Worker, the liturgical movement, and other hallmarks of practical spirituality in this period.

The Catholic revival itself may have been more of a moment than a movement, but many still gaze back at it with admiration and longing. Brown makes a generally positive assessment of the fruits of the Catholic revival but is nevertheless a realistic interpreter of its place in American religious history. He knows that the Second Vatican Council coupled with the "arrival" of Catholics into mainstream American life removed the features that gave the "Catholic renaissance" its distinctive character and its power to shape American Catholic destiny. Like Laurence Moore, Brown realizes that "outsiderhood" gives religious groups a special source of creative energy.[2] With the loss of their identity as a group at some distance from the "secular world," American Catholics in the seventies relinquished the goals of a Catholic "revival" in favor of different strategies of cultural interaction and religious life.

The story of the Grail is, for Brown, a morality play about the Catholic revival. Just as those most active in the projects inspired by the revival eventually realized that their worldview was a "well-intentioned abstraction" that could not work in a pluralistic society, so the Grail was finally "led beyond the bounds of explicit Catholic affiliation." The Grail's story, says Brown, "exemplifies above all the more or less inevitable demise of the Catholic Revival's vision of the Church and world."[3] The bell tolls, therefore, not for the Grail, but for the Catholic revival, of which the Grail was once a significant part.

Where does that leave the Grail movement in the 1990s? Has it "receded to the fringe of the Church and beyond" as Brown suggests?[4] I do not believe so. Brown's conclusions tend to ignore the connections between the Grail and the women's movement, and he fails to place the history of the Grail in any feminist context. He reports rightly that the early years of the Grail were decidedly suspicious of twentieth-century feminism and shows that van Ginneken's hopes for the renewal of the Catholic church lay in the application of stereotypical feminine virtues to a world choked by "masculine" greed and materialism. He captures the naivete of those who were willing to believe that the primary task of women is to inspire men and to bring the spirit of self-sacrifice and charity to a broken world. Members of the Grail movement *did* believe in "feminine potential" and in the need for a special type of training for women in the lay apostolate, but they also believed in stretching women to the limits of their power, one hallmark of the women's movement. The Grail had its own distinctive vision of feminine potential which drew hundreds of women into its orbit. I am not arguing that the Grail's early history was feminist as we would define the term today, but neither is it possible to get a clear reading on this group without more attention to the women's movement than Brown gives it.

Brown believes that the Grail has lost touch with its original intentions. In *New Catholic Women*, I argued to the opposite conclusion, finding today's Grail members faithful to its founding vision.

At the same time, I understand why Brown comes to the conclusions he does. If the original aim of the Grail was to be a women's movement based, not upon feminist principles, but upon the complementary role of women in the church and in the world, then the Grail has changed. If the Grail took a highly traditional approach to organizing young girls and training them to be fervent Catholic women for the purposes of converting the world to Catholicism, then the Grail has clearly strayed from its original path. Of course, so has almost everyone else in the Catholic world: the "original vision" of an overwhelming number of mid-century lay apostolate groups is no longer operating to describe American Catholic life.

The Grail is no longer a youth movement, no longer engaged in missionary activity, no longer working in a national network of city centers. Its goal is not the conversion of the world, and its understanding of Catholicism is no longer based upon the belief that the Catholic church has within it the only answers to the problems of the modern world. Members of the Grail no longer seek to forge a new Christendom by training high-school girls in the paradox of self-denial and womanly strength to accept their special vocations in the world. All of these aspects of Grail identity in the 1950s reflected a particular understanding of Catholicism rooted in a theology of the cross and testified to an acceptance of the complementary status of women in the church.

The development of the Grail's relationship to the modern women's movement has been a long process. From the beginning, the Grail was a movement directed by women. Unlike many orders of sisters whose lives were ultimately directed by Roman congregations or male members of the same branch of religious life, the women of the Grail controlled their own lives and destinies. They operated within the framework of Roman Catholicism and were eager to be obedient and faithful daughters of that church, but they managed to maintain a deeply rooted and somewhat surprising autonomy. They had female spiritual directors and defined themselves in ways that maintained their independence.

The Grail began in Holland in 1921 as an enthusiastic group of women with an interest in liturgy, a flair for the dramatic, and courage that sometimes seemed to go beyond good sense. They first attracted attention by staging massive, colorful rallies and by enacting religious dramas in Amsterdam's Olympic stadium. In the 1930s, hundreds of young Grail members staged countermarches against Hitler youth. Today the Grail has lost some of its youthfulness but none of its enthusiasm. It maintains a lively and creative interest in liturgy and continues to ground its spiritual energy in the events of Holy Week. Some of the most innovative and helpful handbooks of feminist ritual expression within the Catholic tradition have come from Grail members. Linda Clark, Marian Ronan, and Eleanor Walker's *Image-Breaking Image-Building* is a brilliant transformation of religious symbols; Susan Cady, Marian Ronan, and Hal Taussig's *Wisdom's Feast* is a provocative ecumenical project of feminist spirituality.[5]

Grail members today exhibit the same kind of courage and innovative spirit that has characterized the movement for half a century. The old training days have passed, but a new summer program, "The Global Village," attracts high-school girls to Grailville for a week-long workshop led by an intercultural team of women concentrating on issues of justice, ecology, cultural understanding, and religious expression. A program sponsored by the Grail center at Cornwall-on-Hudson offers young women the opportunity for cultural exchange by way of a two-week trip to Mexico and a week-long "integration and evaluation experience" in New York.

The old farm near Loveland, Ohio, is no longer the center of a new agrarian movement as it was when it was associated with some of the rural-life goals of the 1940s. Today a significant portion of the acreage has been turned over to a massive recycling and ecological renewal project involving people from all over the county. Grail members have become active in "permaculture," a word coined by Australian ecologist Bill Mollison to describe a complex set of goals designed to enable humanity to live in harmony with the earth. A series of "earth weekends" in 1990 were offered for Grail members and others who share an ecofeminist vision.

It is true, as Brown says, that Grailville has changed its way of being in the world "from an organization to a meeting place," from a working community of women to a conference center, but I do not think there is as much to mourn in that decision as he does. In a world desperate for reflective space, the attractions of bucolic surroundings and dedicated social involvement say something about the Grail's ability to adapt to new circumstances. Van Ginneken placed his vision in the hands of women because he thought only women had the flexibility to maintain the kind of organization he imagined. If flexibility is one key to assessing steadiness of vision, then the Grail has maintained clear links with its founding principles.

In the 1950s, members of the Grail thought of themselves as instruments of the Holy Spirit in the renewal of the world. Women who spent time in various Grail settings said that they were empowered by their experiences, because they had been challenged to act beyond what was expected for women at the time. Thus, while the early Grail movement in this country addressed creative ways for women to fulfill their expected roles, because members were expected to be living not just as wives and mothers, but as "apostles," the women were able to reach past traditional expectations.

If Grail members in the 1950s were forceful in articulating women's role in the lay apostolate, they are equally forceful today in articulating women's roles in the church, broadly understood, and in the world. With missionary zeal, Grail members were sent all over the world in the 1950s and today still maintain a network of international members. Indigenous Grail teams are located in fifteen different countries and are involved in local attempts to train women for leadership in health care and community development. Grail members at an international level have worked to forge a new theology of women that is at once spiritually rich and politically responsive. They have steadily and consciously moved beyond the language of women's *roles* in a patriarchal world toward an understanding of themselves as active shapers of the world in which they live.

The Grail has had, from the beginning, two related and continually developing goals: to be women-centered and to be Catholic-centered. Their commitment to women at first was grounded in the traditional Catholic teaching that God created human beings with gender-specific roles for women and men. Accordingly, early Grail programs emphasized a special woman's nature and capitalized on specific women's gifts. The commitment to women has not changed, but the supporting foundation is no longer complementarity.

Today's Grail is explicitly feminist in language and in its aims and deeply sensitive to the need women have to listen to one another in a supportive environment. It is possible to trace the history of Catholic feminism in Grail programs in the 1970s and 1980s. Beginning in 1970 with a workshop led by Mary Daly, moving to 1972 with a week-long program, "Women Exploring Theology," and continuing through 1977 with an annual "Seminary Quarter at Grailville," Grail members, feminist critics of church and society, seminary students, and interested women began to examine the texts and ideas of the women's movement as it intersected with the postconciliar church.

One of the characteristics of the women's movement has been its willingness to engage in creative dialogue with those not usually included in the dialectical process. The openness of Grail members to life-affirming initiatives in a variety of places makes the movement's programming objectives very broad. As women committed to a continual search for spiritual depth and effective service in the world, Grail members and others have had unusual opportunities to listen to a chorus of voices. Grail workshops in the 1980s included introductions to neopaganism, holistic health, ecofeminism, new feminist spiritualities, and Native American rituals. Members and others were invited to attend day-long seminars on world economic realities, the lives of third world women, literary and spiritual perspectives of Afro-American women, and the religious dismay of antifeminist women.

One interesting twist on the original vision as articulated by their Dutch Jesuit founder is connected with Goddess religion and neopaganism. Grail members began by arguing that there *was* such a thing as an apostolate for women, something specific for women in the church. They made this argument on the basis of women's unique nature; and they prided themselves on having "shaken the ideas of modern educators on curriculum for women."[6] Their view of women fit hand in glove with the Catholic revival: just as the world needed Catholicism to save it from secularity, the world needed women to save it from the misuse of power. Van Ginneken's idea that "woman is the last fortress of every people" reflects the *zeitgeist* of an earlier time yet, paradoxically, captures part of the feminist perspective of the 1990s. Goddess feminists, ecofeminists, those who subscribe to a belief in primal matriarchies all subscribe to the notion that women are the last hope for the world. The radical feminist position of Riane Eisler's *The Chalice and the Blade*, for example, is strangely akin to some of the traditional rhetoric about women found in the Grail and in other places sixty years ago. [7]

The impact of the women's movement, along with a sensitive ecumenical consciousness, has led the Grail to articulate its religious identity more inclusively in recent years. As Catholics found themselves engaged in interreligious dialogue and those in the women's movement were drawn to explore interactive possibilities with contemporary revivals of paganism, Grail members found themselves in increasingly pluralistic contexts and discussions. Alden Brown sees their decision to include Protestants as formal members as the most profound crisis faced by the Grail in its long history. Once non-Catholic members were accepted, "the assumption of unanimity about the way the *faith* foundation of the Grail was evolving" was clearly challenged. "The Grail could no longer be considered precisely an expression of the lay apostolate." [8] I am not persuaded that Brown has captured the nuances of the complicated and delicate "membership" issues in the Grail, but he does raise a question about the group's relation to Roman Catholicism that needs to be addressed.

The commitment of the Grail to Roman Catholicism has been articulated in a variety of ways over the years. The movement's initial relationship to Catholicism was both traditional and innovative. As noted, Grail members were inspired by the writings of the popes and also welcomed the "new theology" of French and English writers in the 1940s and 1950s. They were able to express themselves in the language of and had close ties to the other groups that constituted the Catholic revival. When the Second Vatican Council challenged

American Catholics to respond to *aggiornamento*, Grail members—
more like members of progressive religious orders than like typical
members of local parishes—were ready. They had been shaped by
the new personalism in catechetics and were schooled in the dynam-
ics of self-reflection. Like many of the religious communities of the
time, Grail members began to think of themselves in new terms and
to question old patterns of formation, personal growth, and community life. Also like religious communities, they underwent ex-
hausting self-studies and engaged in a critical questioning of their
foundations, goals, and desires for the future. Their stated goals at
the end of this process were similar to their original ones: to foster
apostolic holiness, to serve the church, and to take a special interest
in women's lives.[9]

At an international Grail assembly in 1988, Grail members defined themselves as an international faith community who
"strengthen and support one another in our search for God; urge each
other to be open to the Spirit; and work toward transforming our
world into a place of justice, peace and love." Moving within international circles and often working in justice ministries in third world
countries, it is not surprising that the Grail's understanding of its
life in the world combines concern for women and for justice. Grail
members' familiarity with various international contexts has given
them a special perspective on social needs, and their ongoing struggle to deepen their religious understanding has involved them in a
continual process of trusting one another and trusting their own
experience. "The Grail is a process, transplanted to different parts of
the world, therefore not having the answers people took for granted;
the process can require painful changes, but we already see that it is
worthwhile to trust this process," said Grail members at an international assembly in 1979.[10]

As one traces the development of a new understanding of the
Grail's vocation to women, so too one finds a coherent unfolding in
the religious transformation that combines the movement's original
interest in ritual celebration and social activism with some new
strands in theological discourse. The language of liberation theology
expresses some of the religious experience of Grail members. One's

religious identity is, finally, measured by one's ability to reveal God's love for the world in concrete ways. Social justice as a particular way to live the Gospel has always been a significant part of the Grail experience and a formative part of its self-understanding.

The struggle of Grail members to define themselves in Roman Catholic terms eventually gave way to a catholic acceptance of their diversity. Members no longer have to be associated with a particular geographical space or with a specific Grail project. In a parable used to organize the 1987 general assembly, members were urged to find their connections to one another as if united in a "tough spun web." They were to trust in the goodwill of other members and give them space, united as they were in a life meant to contribute toward the transformation of the world. Some members, it was recognized, followed Christ and lived the sacraments, some dwelt in fervent prayer, others were drawn to meditation based on Zen Buddhism. In the cosmos of religious possibility, some found faith evoking symbols in the earth and others sought the wisdom of the Goddess. Each had some special part to play, some "vision of the web of justice."

The most comprehensive statement of the Grail's religious belief was written for the 1988 international meeting. The members of the American Grail agreed that God is "the central mystery of our lives," and that God's compassionate heart has been revealed in the life, death, and resurrection of Jesus. That Christian core, however, does not prevent other articulations. Nor does it solve the problems of ritual interaction:

> At this time in our history we also find some among us who are deeply touched by the Mystery in other ways. When we live and work together, we know through our day-to-day experience that we do stand together on common ground. But when we try to express this sharing in words, we sometimes feel confused. We place our trust in the Spirit, and the Spirit helps us see that our common ground is likewise a common path . . . toward the healing of our world.

Over the past decade, Grail members have recognized the anguish of trying to find the connections between themselves and God, between each other, and between their community and the world. All agree that they have experienced moments of darkness, frustration, and anger, and many interpret these moments as "painful tests of faith." But they "believe that, in spite of all, the desert will finally flower."

Having read their literature, participated in some of their workshops, and visited their farm in Loveland, I have a strong sense of their desire to reach out to others. They live their experiment in a community that is solidly rooted in the past and intrepidly open to change. The more bonds they can forge with women around the world, the more cheerfully they appear to face the future. Their willingness to engage in dialogue with myriad manifestations of the life of the spirit makes them feel more rather than less grounded. If they are moved to celebrate their connections—a way of imagining a common faith—they realize that they "can give thanks, can sing and drum and dance, praise and rejoice, laugh and shout and play together in countless languages and forms."

At its fifty-year mark in the United States, the Grail's members embody a number of different beliefs and have embarked on disparate spiritual journeys. The different diagnoses of their present condition reflect the ideological sensibilities of the interpreters. The historian of the Catholic revival perceives a dying patient, whereas the feminist interpreter sees a new lease on life.

Although Alden Brown ends his book with a challenge to American Catholicism to forge "a vision which engages the contemporary world in all its complexity and which is at the same time self-critical in a positive way," he does not comment as to whether the Grail can meet this challenge.[11] His tacit conclusions are nevertheless negative. But the Grail seems to me to be a community with real promise for the future. Its trust in the leadership potential of women has been part of its identity from the beginning. In a real sense the Grail has always been a "*women's* movement." But its members' understanding of themselves has changed, and it is no longer a *traditional* movement.

Grail members have no desire to return to the strategies of the past and have found in feminism a new source of energy and a new array of needs—physical and spiritual—that must be met with patience, creativity, and innovative programming. If their choices sometimes look strange to outside observers, they know that they always have. People thought it odd that they were engaged in liturgical dance in the late 1940s and now find it strange that they sponsor workshops on psychosynthesis. No matter. Grail members are today what they were fifty years ago, spiritual adventurers whose connection with the mystery of the universe goes beyond what can be articulated in any specific moment.

CALLED TO A NEW LAND

Priestly Possibilities for

Pioneers

I *wrote this essay in 1985 for the tenth anniversary of the Women's Ordination Conference in St. Louis, where I was the keynote speaker. I thought of taking a historical approach that would rehearse the decade of development for the Women's Ordination Conference and end on a celebratory note, but I was not sure where to locate the revelry. Besides, those who asked me to open the conference wanted me to be "realistic" about the issues and to address the future possibilities for women who hoped to be ordained in the Roman Catholic church. I was aware of a struggle among Catholic women over the ordination issue, some holding out for priesthood for women within the traditional church and others urging an end to an ordained priesthood altogether or at least a gathering of communities outside the institution. I wanted to stimulate discussion by presenting the alternatives as dramatically and clearly as possible.*

As I thought about the best way to characterize the positions, I decided to focus on the conflict between hopefulness and despair, a struggle that applies to many women in the church as they encounter different openings and roadblocks in their spiritual lives. I looked for a metaphor that would do justice to moments of crisis while, at the same time, suggesting the possibility of new life. In doing this, I would have to be honest about the price of new life and resist temptations to sink into sentimental rhetoric.

As I look back on the texts and ideas I used to prepare this essay, I find many of the themes that have occupied my work over the past ten years: uses of biblical images, examples from the history of the church, models of courage in the lives of women like Teresa of Avila, appeals to women to trust themselves and to believe that God works in their lives in discernible ways. The pattern I developed in this essay is rather like the old joke that begins, "Well, I have bad news and good news." I begin with the dismal realities of the situation that stress the inexorability of patriarchy and the futility of trusting that the hierarchy will "do something" to alleviate our anguish, and then I try to find some way out of the bleakness through the tradition itself.

I was particularly interested in casting this essay in terms of spiritual development. I hoped to relate the practical aspects of my interpretation to the theological and existential questions we all face when we manage to get in touch with our deepest selves. Since traditional language about spirituality stresses transformation, I began to think in terms of newness and decided that the best metaphor might be that of a new territory. When I looked to the Bible, I found that there were various stories of new lands and new lives to choose from.

I decided to take the most primitive and possibly the most frightening call from God to the ancestors of a new people. The call to Abraham came suddenly and apparently out of nowhere with an urgency and a vague promise of a good outcome. We do not know whether Abraham anguished for years or made an immediate decision; whether Sarah helped or hindered the discussion; or why God chose them and not some other couple. It is not hard to imagine that the call sounded like lunacy: they were being asked to commit cultural suicide, to leave all the moorings of security, support of family and friends, and comforts of home to set off for an unnamed place under the protection of a dimly seen deity.

The call to a new land seemed an apt metaphor to describe the difficult territory of women's ordination. I believed then and believe now that women have no hope of being ordained in the Catholic church as we know it today. The options that present themselves are these: women can join Protestant denominations, wait unavailingly in the Catholic church, give up the desire for ordination altogether, or act on their vocation in communities that are willing to accept them. All of these options seem to be negative choices. Trans-

lated into painful realities they mean that women must abandon their tra-
dition, wait endlessly for nothing, betray their own sense of vocation, or
pursue that vocation in an "excommunicated" state.

Paradoxically, the final option can also be seen as a positive decision, at
once life threatening and life giving. It is, for me, the most appealing even if
it is the most frightening, which is why I chose to describe it in terms of new
territory, new opportunities for creative theological work, and new moments
of self-discovery on the spiritual journey. This radical choice differs from the
other three: it is not an abandonment of one's own tradition, not a life sentence
to futile longing, and not a relinquishment of one's dreams. It is, rather, a
risky response in faith to a possible call from God to go beyond the borders of
our present experience into a new spiritual land.

If women who want to celebrate the sacraments are being called to a new
land, they are also being invited to an experience of God that goes beyond the
limiting categories of patriarchy. I identify, briefly, new attributes of God
that I think can be found in this new land, dimensions of the divine that I
have found in process thought and adumbrated in parts of the mystical tra-
dition. The God encountered in this new land is a disturbing and deeply
present divine being who helps us on our way and prods us to venture on.

One of the astonishing features of God's call to Abraham and Sarah
was its gratuitousness: out of the clear blue and for no discernible
reason, Abraham and Sarah received an invitation they did not understand. Their positive response to divine initiative made it possible
for Jews, Christians, and Muslims to participate in the search for
transcendence that in part characterizes the Western religious tradition. According to the Bible, God asked Abraham and Sarah to
leave the house of their fathers in order to go to a new land, there to
become a new people.[1] Women seeking ordination to the priesthood
in the Catholic church may also find themselves called away from the
house of their fathers. The "new land," however, may be more spiritual than geographical, more an act of redefinition than a leaving
behind of cherished traditions.

As I explore the history of the women's ordination issue and try to imagine the future in its light, I find myself in an interpretive framework described by two contrasting perspectives.[2] On one side is the despair of the late Marjorie Tuite, and on the other the defiant hopefulness of Elisabeth Schüssler Fiorenza.[3] In the late 1970s, a group of American Catholic bishops sponsored a "dialogue" with selected feminists and activists. At the end of that process—which Rosemary Ruether characterized as a "non-meeting of minds"—an exhausted Tuite told a group assembled in Indianapolis, "They don't want us. They have never wanted us. And they never will want us!" In the early 1980s, Elisabeth Schüssler Fiorenza published *In Memory of Her*, a feminist reading of New Testament theology.[4] Her stunning reinterpretation of early Christianity concluded with the new Good News that women are not marginal in the Jesus movement and need not accept marginal positions in the contemporary church.

Both of these observations are true of women's experience in the Catholic church, and their contradictions challenge my attempts to find a way out of the current ordination crisis. The ability to live within the tension created by the constant exasperation and need to persevere requires the "wisdom of serpents and the innocence of doves," a strategy Jesus himself once suggested to a ragtag group of disciples embarking on their own ministry.

A significant number of Catholic women believe that they are called to priesthood in the Catholic church. In their hearts and in the minds of their supporters, they have clear vocations to sacerdotal ministry that have been tested, schooled, and made available to an institution that denies them, even in theory. The paradox of the situation is very painful: they have been reared in a church with unlimited spiritual possibilities but have been rejected by its fundamental canons. Some may believe that there is reason to hope for change in the contingencies of the moment. Some believe, for example, that the current shortage of priests might eventually open an avenue for women's ordination so that what was once forbidden can become the source of new life in the community. Those who cherish such hopes need to take a hard look at the institution. Hope, like desire, can be extinguished quickly by a careful (or even casual) reading of recent Vatican pronouncements.

Is the Situation Hopeless?

It appears as if Marjorie Tuite was right: "They don't want us!" Church authorities have made that clear in every conceivable way. By ignoring the opinions of most Scripture scholars who see no convincing case against women's ordination in the New Testament, ecclesiastical officials continue to cite Scripture as a primary reason for denying ordination to women. By refusing to submit the misogynist pronouncements of "the Fathers" to a critical exegesis, ecclesiastical officials continue to appeal to tradition as if it should obliterate any desire women might have for priesthood. By espousing a religious form of sex-role stereotyping in the theory of complementarity, the Roman Catholic church can continue to give rhetorical support to the equality of the sexes while treating women as spiritually inferior, ritually unclean, and morally unfit for the ministry of the altar.

Realistically, from my perspective as a historian, the desire for priesthood must be lived within the wrenching reality that women are not wanted within the Roman Catholic church so long as they voice a desire for ordination. Pragmatic understandings of the times we are living in provide another bit of context. For example, the present pope has recently declared Pius IX (1846–1878) "Venerable," which means that the most intransigent pontiff of modern times is presented to us as one in the company of the saints, indeed, one who may himself reach the ranks of the canonized.

Interestingly, Pius IX began his career in the mid nineteenth century as the choice of the liberals. Following the dismal pontificate of Gregory XVI (1830–1846), the urbane, sophisticated Pius began his reign by declaring political amnesty, emptying the Vatican jails, and otherwise thrilling those who hoped that the Roman Catholic church would begin to take its place in the modern world. Within a few years of his coronation, however, caught up in the disruption of

Italian revolutions and forced to flee from Rome disguised as a parish priest, Pius IX had a radical change of heart. For the rest of his reign, which lasted longer than any in history, he made war against modernity. He is remembered for publishing the Syllabus of Errors (1864), declaring the doctrine of the Immaculate Conception, and consolidating the power of the papacy in the doctrine of papal infallibility.[5]

It seems sensible to read the "Venerable" status of Pius IX as a key to the mentality of Pope John Paul II. We might also put it into the context of curtailment that is presently a characteristic of Vatican policies. A recent series of Vatican actions has targeted nuns and priests in political office who hold left-wing views; liberation theologians; modern European theologians, especially those associated with the publication *Concilium*; priests and nuns who have dedicated themselves to ministry to the gay community; and contemplative nuns who oppose some of the medieval constraints of papal cloister. In this context, the willingness to ordain reactionary Anglican ministers while denying married Catholic priests any official role in the service of the church is part of a program; and the campaign to remove women from seminaries as teachers, students, or spiritual directors makes exquisite sense.

It is this combination of things that led Marjorie Tuite to abandon any hope for the ordination of women. Denial of ordination to women is only logical in a church with this specific list of policies. "They do not want us," said Tuite, but we did not need her to bring us that information. The texts, traditions, and canons of Catholicism are relentlessly sexist; liturgical celebration is marred by discriminatory language and practice; pastoral concern is often either oblivious to "women's problems" or hostile to any desire for female empowerment within the church; and the very structures of the institution may well be intractable where women's desire for ordination is concerned.

The past tradition, the present climate, and the presumed future are not hopeful. The path of least resistance, one taken by many women who have been called to ordination, calls for a relinquishing of their Catholicism. Many women have left the Roman Catholic church in order to be ordained as Protestant ministers or Anglican priests. Since denominational background often functions as a kind of ethnic identification that is virtually impossible to escape, I wonder how former Catholic women now serving as Protestant ministers are faring. Furthermore, since we know from our Protestant sisters that the grass is really *not* greener on the other side of the fence—churches that allow ordination of women often have terrible problems finding a job for them since few churches appear to want a "woman minister"—I wonder how many former Catholic women are actually serving as pastors in Protestant churches.

Between a Rock and a Hard Place

What of women who have chosen to remain within the Roman Catholic church in search of an affirmation of their priestly vocations? Their lives can be described in terms of an old adage, caught between a rock and a hard place. The rock is Peter, the symbol of an unmovable papacy and a calcified tradition. The hard place is the call to a new territory of a nonsexist community, for by answering that call, by claiming their vocations in actions of celebration and reconciliation, they will be vilified from many quarters. Women who want to celebrate the sacraments can remain within traditional Catholicism in a state of permanent disappointment (the rock of rejection) or they can claim their priesthood in nontraditional communities, effectively severing their connections with orthodoxy (the hard place of heresy).

I am describing what I believe to be the reality of the situation. Those who remain within traditional Catholicism expecting a change are doomed to disappointment: they will have to relinquish their desire for ordination or attempt to live in a place where nourishment for that desire is constantly dwindling. Those who claim their vocations by taking the radical step of choosing to celebrate the sacraments in nontraditional communities will either be ignored (if they operate quietly) or officially excommunicated (if they or someone else calls attention to what they are doing). Some may counter my interpretation by saying that the Catholic church is changing. But as I understand Catholic church history, the rock will not budge: orthodoxy is the historical rule, not the exception. Periods of "liberalism" are usually followed by periods of "conservatism," and it is safe to say that the liberal spirit of Vatican II has given way to a new conservatism. In the present climate, no doors will open for women priests.

I am not inclined to be so negative, however, about the "hard place." I have imagined it as a new land where women are called to find new ways to be faithful to God's designs. This new land may not be as forbidding as it looks on first glance: scouts have been there, outposts have been established, towns are springing up, and word is that they need the liturgical leadership of women.

A life attuned to the Spirit demands a willingness to embrace vocations despite official opposition. Those who are called to push for major structural change within Catholicism will be pursuing a course that will widen human possibilities in an institution ostensibly dedicated to mediating divine generosity. Of course, no one takes on such a task without models, and it is extremely helpful to share stories of innovation and empowerment. In other words, women who decide to respond to the call to set out for this new land need support groups.

In the context of those groups, it is possible to do a revisionary reading of the lives of heroic women in the Roman Catholic tradition to see how they managed to get what they wanted in a context that denied them any power. Catherine of Siena, for example, managed to lead an influential life by refusing the traditional choices of her society—marriage or a convent—and so found in her singleness a powerful vocation. Teresa of Avila, confident that she heard the voice of God within her, used it to set in motion an enormously important reform movement at a time when contemplative prayer was under suspicion and when spirited women were submitted to constant regulation. Remembering these strong women and others, we have reason to think that we, too, might reach beyond the present limits to change the system.

Women on the verge of venturing out into new territory *can* find strength in Jesus. Whether or not he can be described as the leader of a countercultural movement, Jesus' attitudes toward women were essentially positive and empowering: women were not meant to be marginal participants in the church and should resist those officials who attempt to push them to the fringes of their own tradition.[6] Elisabeth Schüssler Fiorenza's work poses this rhetorical question: Who stands in the authentic stream of the Jesus movement? Members of a patriarchal hierarchy bent on preserving the status quo, or those who understand the prophetic, God-driven words and life of Jesus as equalitarian, antiestablishment, politically subversive, and open to radical change?

Roman Catholic feminist theologians have begun to make it possible for Catholic women to reimagine the church on their own terms, and the Womenchurch movement has begun to provide a setting in which Catholic women along with their Protestant sisters can experience the power of the Gospel in a new, self-created space. Those women who describe themselves in exile from patriarchy deny the smothering misogyny of the traditions and texts in order to celebrate the stories that valorize women. Those who continue to be part of the institutional church but long for some supplemental liturgies and alternative sources of spiritual support begin to get in touch with their own strengths and to feel the stirrings of the spirit in the collective voices of women.

One key to power is the refusal to accept the idea that God somehow wills the subordination of women. Empowered by the Gospel and by the collective support of the women's movement, it is possible to resist a conservative reading of traditional stories. According to Schüssler Fiorenza, the equalitarian ethics of Jesus, his behavior and words, were distorted by those who made the final selection of New Testament texts and by those who subsequently interpreted them.[7] There has also been a male editing of the church's traditions. Feminists engaged in a rereading of medieval history can show us that stories of Catherine and Teresa were transformed into guidelines for submissiveness by those who focused on their obedience or on their penitential practices and who therefore muted their radical willfulness and self-assertive spirituality.

It is not unimaginable that hostile interpreters of the women's movement in the church will characterize "Womenchurch" as the AntiChrist. It is not inconceivable that women seeking ordination or gathering for alternative liturgies will be condemned by institutional authorities. Those seeking ordination within the Catholic church have already suffered the pains of rejection. Those standing in solidarity with women who have vocations but no immediate outlets for fulfilling them also experience frustration. All, however, have a pressing vocation to something different from priesthood. Our task, as Rosemary Ruether reminds us, is to unmask distortions, to call the church to the accountability of prophetic messianism. Our power, as Elisabeth Schüssler Fiorenza shows us, is the revelatory strength of women's lives to resist any attempt to read us out of our own tradition even as we act to change its structural life.

The situation is simple and confrontational: ecclesiastical officials do not want us, but they cannot get rid of us. As Mary Bader Papa said some years ago, the pedestaled promises of traditional Catholic teaching are not meant for "bad girls, poor girls, and independent women."[8] Vatican bureaucrats appeal to "the teaching of the church" in order to deny power to women, yet those same women can claim to be faithful to Catholic tradition when they insist that the church is a discipleship of equals. However empowered women may feel as they read their tradition in a new light, the realities of power within the institutional church caution against any kind of celebration of ourselves. Women in the Catholic church have no vote and precious little voice. We look with sober realism at the sexist church we live in, knowing that neither our own stories, nor radical women saints, nor even the example of Jesus has been enough to countermand the stifling moves of the patriarchy.

One does not have to feel called to priestly ordination in order to feel frustrated in today's church. Women who have embraced traditional roles either have to cast a blind eye to the social changes for women in the world around them or they have to use a significant portion of their liturgical energy ignoring sexist language and discriminatory practices in the church. Many Catholic women have to explain to their daughters that they might one day be a justice of the Supreme Court but never a priest; in searching for an explanation of that ban, they will confront a tradition that both honors and humiliates women. They live in a country where Title 9 legislation has made women's sports an exciting reality, so that they may be rooting for Eddie's softball team on Tuesdays and Suzy's on Thursdays; but they will attend a church where Suzy has to sit with her mother in a pew on Sunday while Eddie is welcomed on the altar as a server. Every Mother's Day, "Father" will tell them about motherhood and they can bask in the glow of a tradition that elevates the idea of womanhood while it denies power to real women and stifles their potential. If in this sad scenario cognitive dissonance sets in, who can be surprised? Cognitive dissonance is the disruption of one's framework of perception by a jarring encounter with another one: finally we all come to a point where the old system simply does not make sense anymore. It is here, in this tragic place, full of anger and desire, frustration and hope, that we all must learn to survive.

In many ways the ordination question puts Catholic women in a crisis situation, trying to find ways to preserve the best parts of their own tradition while working to dismantle the oppressive consequences of sexism within it. Although feminist theologians and those involved in the Womenchurch movement have taken this task as their own, it may not appeal to other Catholic women, and may seem especially threatening to those who desire ordination. Those who believe they have vocations to the priesthood may see a denial of their life's hope in what may well be the inescapable political consequences of being a woman in today's church.

I am not suggesting that anyone eschew a priestly vocation in order to throw their pastoral energy into politics, but I am convinced that one effective means of survival, one way to move creatively into the future, lies in choosing to remain inside the tradition in order to disclaim its patriarchal actions. Another avenue of resistance, of course, is to withdraw from the institution. Some women who feel called to ordination and experience increasing frustration in their desire are claiming power for themselves by finding and responding to priestly missions among women and men who need them.

As Virginia Woolf said in *A Room of One's Own* and as Mary Daly echoed in *Beyond God the Father*, we have to have the exhilarating experience of becoming ourselves rather than reflecting men back to themselves at twice their actual size.[9] If we can do that, if we can really see ourselves as authentic bearers of the Jesus tradition, as those called to a discipleship of equals, called to celebrate the supper of the Lord and to minister to the downtrodden of the world, then we will already be doing something terribly radical. Just in knowing who we are, we will create an upheaval of epic proportions, we will throw the whole system off balance, and we will seriously challenge the future of patriarchal Christianity.

Breaking Boundaries

Claiming power as legitimate ministers in the church puts Catholic women in a position to confront large theological and existential questions. Our confrontation with sexism in the church gives us new ways to understand existence and abandonment, life and death. Some interpreters say that human beings deny death precisely because they cannot bear to admit their own contingency. Faced with the possibility of obliteration, human beings reject death and build in its place an idolatrous self-image. I wonder if I might apply this image to the patriarchal church. The idea that men alone can preside over the Eucharist has been created by males for their own glorification and to deny their own contingency. It demands that women's hopes for empowerment be continually thwarted. But fidelity to the Jesus traditions demands that we oppose this image of church by reaching for the fullness of life promised in the Gospels.

The desire for ordination can also be linked to large theological questions of existence. If we can define desire, not as an emptiness waiting to be filled, but as a fullness waiting for activation, then women's desire for ordination is an event waiting to happen. Furthermore, since modern theologians suggest that the fulfillment of a desire opens people to transcendence, women's ordination will open new human possibilities and eventually lead to God.

Whenever I search for God in the modern world, I end up in the medieval world. Far from finding medieval religious culture forbidding, I usually find comfort in it and also ideas that help me. For example, the notion that the image of God lies within us in order to awaken a lost memory of our true selves helps me to be more confident about my true self. The scholastic understanding of the soul as the seat of intellect and will, based on the belief that the soul's function was to mirror Godself back to the deity in a unique way, leads to some thought about my own uniqueness. Since creation makes all of us the bearers of our own facet of an unlimited divine personality and urges each nature to reflect that icon back to its source as brilliantly as possible, one can argue that God needs all creatures to be as fully themselves as possible. The roots of such an interpretation are fully biblical: the implications of the partnership imagery of the Bible point us toward a union between God and ourselves that enriches both partners beyond their abilities to achieve alone.

What if priesthood for women is itself a unique imaging of God that reflects a fuller understanding of the divine personality? What if the God we believe to be infinitely larger than and more complex than the patriarchal church would have us imagine has a stake in women priests? What if the denial of that unique vocation by the patriarchy is a temptation against the obligations we all have to become our best and truest selves? Perhaps those who are called to ordination have vocations to resistance. Perhaps women's priesthood must be built upon a refusal to acknowledge the blasphemous, nonpriestly image that the patriarchal church projects upon women.

I believe that women in the Catholic church, including those who seek ordination, must refuse to abide by the current limitations of that church while actively celebrating the mysteries made available to us from the tradition. If the Roman Catholic church will not "grant" ordination to women, then perhaps they have to find their own ways to respond to God's invitations by courageous acts and daring refusals.

First of all, we must refuse to shore up the patriarchal church. We must let the old system die. We can no longer jump into the breach to fill the gaps left by the priest shortage but must consistently refuse to minister unless we are recognized as women with authentic vocations in the church. It is time to quit fooling ourselves about our "ministry" when it means that we are permitted to do the work but have no power to change things. It is time to quit being "Father's helper" in a church that considers women unfit to celebrate the Eucharist.

Women must learn to minister on their own terms, recognizing that even within the present system some are called to specific functions. It is not unheard of that some nonclerical spiritual directors sometimes "forgive sins" and otherwise participate in "priestly" life. Likewise, some women celebrate the Eucharist with small groups, calling it a "para-liturgy." It is time to use the old language as our new language. I believe that women who celebrate these mysteries can call them sacraments. Perhaps it is more clearly an act of love than a gesture of defiance to look for ways to exercise a vocation to priesthood in the context of a self-gathered community of equals.

In reviewing Edward Schillebeeckx's controversial book, *Ministry*, Ralph Keifer said that "reformation . . . requires a simultaneous crisis of liturgy, authority, spirituality and doctrine as its preconditions. It also requires the emergence of the practical (and intellectually defensible) alternatives to the existing ecclesiastical structures."[10] I believe we have reached that crisis point and that one of the practical and intellectually defensible alternatives to existing structures is the claiming of the priestly vocation by women.

As Rosemary Ruether said at the first Women's Ordination Conference more than fifteen years ago, "We must demystify the power of the priesthood."[11] Sacramental power is not something owned by priests but something invested in the believing community. Women with vocations can minister to a gathered community, celebrate the Eucharist with them, participate in rituals that bear God's loving reconciliation to sinners, and find ways in the context of that group to minister to the world. Such priestly actions need to be done not as a hidden ceremony outside the church, but as a witness to new life and subversive action within the church.

Women's claims to power lie in their relationship to the life and work of Jesus, and in the needs of a new community. The Roman Catholic church now has a sizable community of women who can no longer find nurturance in their parish churches but who continue to identify themselves as Catholics because they need and want the sacraments. It is courageous and fitting to hear in their need and from the depths of their pain a call to legitimate ordination. In order to respond to such a call, those who desire a priestly venue need to remember that they cannot be marginalized by illegitimate laws or appeals to "the church's teaching" when that teaching, as Schüssler Fiorenza says, cannot claim the example of Jesus to legitimate its praxis. Women called to ordination therefore must celebrate the Eucharist openly as part of their heritage within Catholicism.

I have no doubt that some will find these subversive suggestions disturbing. Many believe that vocations exist solely within the confines of the church as we know it today, and the idea of celebrating the Eucharist without the official permission of the church, without traditional ordination, seems clearly heretical, or, at the least, counterproductive. I wonder, however, if it is possible to be a "woman priest" within the present system without contributing to the very structures that have oppressed women throughout Christian history. If we look at women professionals in every field, we see that success is often measured by how well a particular woman has been able to conform to the rules and expectations of the patriarchal institution, whether that institution is a law firm, a university, or an ecclesiastical body.

The logic of our internal development suggests that when we respond to challenges, we are changed into something greater than ourselves. There is therefore every possibility that the people of God can become something greater than themselves through the radical transformation of images and structures evidenced in women's ministry. Attempting to fit one's gifts into unjust structures corrupts the symbols and diminishes their transformative power. I am thus not persuaded that ordination within the present system can ever be a good idea either for an individual woman or for the people of God.

Pioneers in a New Territory

Fortunately or unfortunately, women who desire ordination in the Catholic church are called into new territory in the historical and psychological landscape of Roman Catholicism. Such women are pioneers, and no one in her right mind really wants to be one. As Joan Huber said many years ago in describing the women's movement, "A person who maintains a self-definition with no social support is mad; with a minimum of support, a pioneer; and with broad support, a lemming. Most of us are lemmings. We accept or change our ideas of our own rights and duties only when we perceive the social support for doing so."[12] In the new territory, whether that place is called Womenchurch or is simply a new dimension of the religious imagination, a woman's vocation will be lived out in the pioneering spirit. Even if women find the social support to exercise their priesthood, that support will not take away all the fears of the unknown that pioneers must meet, nor reduce the risks of their special calling.

Given the circumstances we now live in, a woman who believes she has a vocation to the priesthood is by definition involved in a political struggle. I suspect those who are called to priesthood have felt this even though many may want with all their might to deny it. It is time to stop dreaming that "they" will do something for us or that the priest shortage will work on women's behalf. A Catholic woman with a call to ordination cannot afford to be blind to the communities that need her now. I wonder if the pain of the church's denial of ordination might be overcome by claiming priestly vocations in a simple, direct way? I wonder if it is possible for women to live out the call to priesthood without being silenced by an appeal to prudence? A vocation to the priesthood, after all, is an invitation to reflect on one's relationship to God and to the church.

Make no mistake. If women act on their vocations within the institution as I have suggested, the institution will try to disown them. The "slings and arrows of outrageous fortune" will be nothing compared with the rejection from family, acquaintances, and ecclesiastical officials. Painful as it is, we must remain fully conscious of the hostility that the very question of women's ordination engenders in some people. The Roman Catholic church is not designed for women who refuse to accept secondary status: it is a patriarchal institution that continues to define woman's nature as "complementary" to man's, and its restrictions are based on a belief that women are, at some very fundamental level, inferior to men. When I quote Marjorie Tuite—"they do not want us"—I am talking about those who discourage feminists, ignore "women's problems," and deny ordination to women gifted with a call to priestly ministry. We have some choices in the face of this reality, one of which is to see that *their* not wanting us frees us to minister to those who do.

As inheritors of the Jesus tradition, we can confront the denials of those who condemn our choices as outrageous or counterproductive. If the phrase "they do not want us" is troublesome, we can begin by asking who *they* are and by remembering who *we* are. Then, without leaving the church, we can begin to minister to that growing group of women whose hunger for spiritual nourishment and for the ministry of women is almost palpable. As women with an alternative vision rooted in the emancipatory praxis of the early Jesus community, we can reclaim the center of the tradition in a number of ways. Catholic feminists do it by participating in the Womenchurch movement. Women seeking ordination who do not want to join a Protestant church might claim their power by celebrating the Eucharist and participating in rituals of reconciliation.

I have already suggested that there are people out there waiting for ministry. Women under forty are leaving the church in unprecedented numbers, and their mothers may not be far behind them. Is there not a legitimate call to ordination from those women whose hearts are filled with rage and pain? Can women longing for ordination not provide a supplemental liturgy for those who cannot yet leave the parish, but whose experience there is not life giving? At a more radical level, can they not imagine providing an alternative for those women who will not attend a parish but whose needs are rooted in the Catholic sacramental system? Whatever the answers to these questions, I know that finally each person must take courage from the God we know to be inadequately represented in the present symbols of our faith. In refusing to serve the patriarchy, we begin to serve a God who is related, persuasive, and involved, and whose reality is much broader and deeper than we have been led to believe. A divine being whose modus operandi is disturbing the peace and calling us to new life, whose love is made available as freely as bread is broken and wine is drunk, is calling: "Leave your fathers' house and go to a new place."

SPRINGS OF WATER IN A DRY LAND

A Process Model of Feminist Spirituality

This essay was originally written for a symposium in Portland, Oregon, in 1987 and later revised for the Theology Institute at Villanova University. The generic problem at its center is the same one that has been vexing me for years: how to respond constructively to the anguish of Catholic women who can no longer define themselves in traditional terms but who cannot bring themselves to leave their church behind. In this case, I decided to try to formulate some attributes of feminist spirituality in terms of process theology.

In 1985, at the Women's Ordination Conference in St. Louis, I raised some points of process thought that I found attractive and potentially useful for feminist spirituality. I tried to soften the terrors of a "new land" somewhat by referring to new attributes of God to be discovered once women left "their fathers' house" behind. I wanted to build on some of those themes in this essay, especially the ones pertaining to "a new God."

The language of novelty in relation to God is frightening and a little misleading. In fact, one of my main goals here is to show that the attributes of the process God, albeit minor themes in the biblical tradition, have always been there. We are not inventing God: the minor harmonies of the biblical tradition can be shown to anticipate and resonate with the themes of process theology. The reason I am attracted to the God of process thought and not to Goddess theology has much to do with my need for context, to be grounded. I *am rooted in historical evidence: if I cannot locate something in Scripture or tradition or history, I am not attracted to it. In order to address general issues of feminist spirituality from a process perspective, I wanted to build upon biblical themes and show how they could work as a basis for this "new God."*

Although I find process theology comforting and attractive, I am quite aware that the attributes of the process God are disconcerting to those who are at home with the traditional characteristics of the divine being. Rather than a God who is in total control of all outcomes, the God of process thought depends upon our choices and grows in understanding and relatedness along with the rest of us. Years ago when I was describing the differences to a Catholic friend, she said bluntly, "Well, if God is not in charge of every-thing, then I say to hell with it."

My relationship to process thought came through a gradual refinement of my own spiritual needs. Since my preconciliar Catholic background and my attraction to the writings of sixteenth-century mystics tended to define spiri-tuality for me in essentially private terms, I was both attracted to and repelled by liberation theology when I first encountered it nearly twenty years ago. Because liberation theology is a politically informed theological perspective that locates God's present activity in the lives of marginalized peoples, I found it a valuable corrective to my introverted piety. Since it is based on a radical rereading of biblical texts and interprets the work of Jesus in dramatic new ways, it challenged me to become more involved in the world around me, more sensitive to poverty and marginalization, and more aware of present locations of divine revelation.

My encounters with liberation theology were not altogether satisfying, however. I am not persuaded that the essentially third world perspective of liberationists works well in a first world context. As a way to break through the old dichotomy between work and prayer, liberation theology helped me to consider spirituality in different terms, but it also left me wondering how to gather my own particular needs together with new ideas. I found myself longing for something more metaphysical.

I turned to process thought to find a way to combine my own spiritual inclinations with insights from modern theologians. If spirituality can be defined as contemplation in action, then how do we root ourselves in contem-plation? Do we look for God in prayer? Wait for a contemplative moment that is essentially secret and dependent upon quiet watchfulness? Or do we look for God in the events of our lives and then hope to find God in prayer? I have not solved this riddle for myself, but my tendency, when I cannot figure out where to find God, is to be patient and let God find me.

I turn so regularly to Teresa of Avila and am also attracted to process theology because in both cases God longs for relationship with humanity in general and individuals in particular. In process theology, devised by and from the work of Alfred North Whitehead, God is described as longing for and actually needing *human responsiveness and creativity. In this essay, then, I decided to focus on divine longing as a way to ameliorate the anguish many Catholic women feel in terms of their own religious lives.*

In contrast with some of my other work that begins with a painful recounting of the present moment, I begin here with the comforting words of Yahweh to a people oppressed by exile. It looks to me as if the author of Second-Isaiah has radically and deliberately reinterpreted a traditional theme of Hebrew spirituality—the ancient wilderness story—to suit the needs of a suffering people. I suggest that Catholic women, suffering within the limitations of a patriarchal church, are effectively stranded in a desert and challenged to imagine a new future for themselves as they trust God to re-create them. The re-creative modes of Second-Isaiah, the new songs demanded by Yahweh, fit the image I have of women in the wilderness. New songs and new life are like promises of water in a dry land.

In the moving passages that begin Second-Isaiah, the prophet speaks the words that Handel would later set so magnificently to music in the *Messiah*: "Comfort my people, . . . speak tenderly to them, . . . I will make the wilderness a pool of water and the dry land springs of water." Although these heavily messianic texts were later used by Christians to interpret the life and work of Jesus, they had a different meaning for postexilic Jews. In order to comfort a thoroughly demoralized people, the author of Second-Isaiah made a radical reinterpretation of the ancient wilderness traditions of the exodus story. I believe that many Christian feminists are in the process of trying to redefine the desert for themselves, as the author of Second-Isaiah did for his constituency.

Images of Wilderness

Although the original exodus did not lead to Jerusalem, the author of Second-Isaiah says that now the people will walk through the waters, parted by God's powerful hand, and march, joyfully, to Zion, singing all the way (Isa. 51:9–13). The original exodus experience contains stories about thirst and the need for water, but they are stories of rebellion as well as comfort (Exod. 17; Num. 20; Deut. 32, 48, 52), whereas the water images in Second-Isaiah reflect the lavish tenderness of the deity. The later biblical author thus used the most ancient and sacred texts of his tradition to create something new. He was able to give meaning to his own situation by revising the old story of conflict and abandonment into a song of nurturance and delight. In so doing, he re-created the wilderness and gave the desert a new, celebratory meaning.

The original exodus was a troubled time: people were dramatically rescued from oppression only to be plunged into an experience of community and expectation that they claimed to find more oppressive than the Egyptian slavedrivers from whom they had just escaped. When they believed they were dying of thirst and cried out for water, their needs were heard as complaints and their thirst understood as a metaphor for insatiability. The wilderness, as remembered in the book of Numbers, was a harsh place, and the contentious wanderers were apparently faithless, rebellious, and occasionally the objects of divine wrath.

The Isaian wilderness, on the other hand, was a *new* desert. There people were nurtured by God and reminded of the loving deeds of creation; they were brought back from the abysmal experiences of the exile and promised a new life in a new Jerusalem. They were encouraged to "sing a new song" and to put on beautiful garments. A new revelation unfolds in the poetry of the author: we meet a God who suffers with people, who comforts and serves, who persuades and responds. The Isaian reinterpretation, coming as it does after the destruction of Jerusalem, encourages people to rekindle their dreams and renew their trust in divine faithfulness. It makes it possible to believe in the future, to outstare the emptiness of the exile with the determined belief that still to come is a time in which all things will be made new.

Whether contemporary Christian feminists consider themselves to be in exile from their homeland or on an adventurous escape from the land of the Pharaohs, they may find it useful to remember that beneath their fears and blindness, the liberated slaves maintained a conviction that God *was*, somehow, guiding them to the promised land and that the promises of a new Jerusalem grounded the hopes of the Jewish exiles. Christian feminists may need to hold onto these stories because their own wilderness experiences are very real.

No longer "at home" in the oppressive land of Egypt, we cannot return there however much we may long for its savory dishes and its familiar ways. At the same time, in exile from our religious tradition, we cannot yet see the "new Jerusalem" and so often find it hard to go forward with much confidence. Many women feel abandoned by a divine being who has brought us to a morbid place where there seems to be neither food nor water. And if we do find solace in the promise of something new, it may be an ambivalent kind of comfort. Like the Hebrews who felt that they had to choose between dying in a wasteland or returning to slavery and oppression, our choices may appear to be bleak: religious alternatives are not yet clear, or if clear, not congenial, and our own tradition is forbiddingly painful.

The Hebrews were alienated, oppressed, enslaved, and finally forced to flee in order to preserve their lives. Many women in the Catholic church, when they discover the misogynist heritage of their own tradition, suffer profound alienation as well. They experience the liturgy as fundamentally oppressive since it appears to betray the God of their deepest desire. In realizing how dramatically the parish structure depends upon the goodwill of the pastor and, at the same time, living under the direction of an insensitive or hostile priest, women know something of enslavement. The double bind they find themselves in forces them to choose between survival on someone else's terms or survival on their own.

Many flee to what I am calling the wilderness. Although this desert does not appear to be a life-giving place, it may well be a life-discovering place. Contemporary women, like the Hebrews before them, can remember the covenant and hope that they will find the promised land. Failing that, exiled women, like the Jews addressed by Second-Isaiah, can gather in the desert to sing a new song and anticipate something radically new.

The Experience of Alienation

The texts, traditions, language, pastoral care, and structures of Catholicism devalue women. Even when that devaluation is not explicit, it cannot be denied. One need only recall that before the women's movement began to have an impact on Catholicism, almost everything we read about ourselves—about our natures, aspirations, and sources of fulfillment—was written by male celibates. Paradigmatically, women were either subservient, ennobling creatures like Mary or independent temptresses like Eve. Behind this schizophrenic view of women lay centuries of misogynist writing that avoided real women by resorting to mystification or vituperation.

Beneath the rhetoric about Mary and motherhood, Catholic feminists discovered a deep well of prejudice against women. In the texts and laws of the church, women are said to be naturally unclean, spiritually dubious, unfit for service on the altar, intellectually inferior to men, dangerously seductive in youth, and garrulous in old age. Virtually all of this demeaning material has been presented as God's will and has been used to justify the religious form of sex-role stereotyping known as complementarity. Since God created women as inferior beings, designed to complete men, so the reasoning goes, church teaching is bound to uphold and perpetuate the natural order of things by replicating the divine design. The literature and assumptions of Catholicism about women therefore assume divinely willed differences that relegate women to secondary positions. In other words, they alienate women.

Oppression and Enslavement

In the weekly experience of liturgy and the ongoing life of women in the parish, oppression is real and very painful. In the few studies that ask women to name their own experience in the parish, it is clear that women still working within the church structure feel invisible, powerless, unwelcome, and trivialized.[1] They hear the sexist language of the liturgy as rejecting or hostile, and many believe that the church's refusal to ordain women is a reminder of division and inequality. Those women who manage to maintain a hopeful attitude in this situation admit to being tired. They feel drained by their work for a church that fails to nourish them. They are oppressed even in situations where they are working in some kind of ministry.

Furthermore, just as the Hebrews were subject to the will of Pharaoh, women are in bondage to the views and personal styles of their pastors. Those who are happy in their present parish can only hope that their bishop will make no personnel changes, whereas those who currently endure a misogynist pastor can only pray fervently that a new priest will make their lives better. Whether parish styles emphasize organization, social action, teaching, service, ethnicity, hospitality, or sacramental activity, the main character is still the pastor.[2] The climate for women in the church, therefore, is set by the attitudes and behavior of members of the clergy.

Many women have difficult interactions with their priests and struggle to define the sources of their discontent. Some of them acknowledge that general cultural formation leads to male insensitivity toward women, and others blame seminary training and enforced celibacy; but most feel that priests are simply uninterested in and unprepared to deal with family violence, rape, divorce, unwanted pregnancy, single parenting, birth control, abortion, widowhood, and other so-called women's issues.

These experiences force Catholic women to choose between oppression and exile. If they stay within the structure, they are defined as secondary beings and given only tasks appropriate to those at the bottom of the hierarchical ladder. They may have relatively more status in these days of vocational crisis—for example, women might be serving as parish administrators in some cases—but they still operate under male direction and have no real power within the institution. Those who embrace traditional roles and structures have to cast a blind eye to the social changes for women in the world around them: they are in bondage to an identity that has been decreed for them.

Those who simply try to survive in spite of the hardships, who are not happy where they are but have nowhere else to go, have to use a significant portion of their liturgical energy ignoring sexist language, discriminatory practices, and the denial of women's talents, ideas, and power within the church. Whether or not middle-aged women can accept traditional explanations for inferior status is not so important as whether their daughters will. Beneath resigned acceptance, therefore, is the real possibility that subsequent generations will not benefit from it. Such is the life of those who remain in the land of the Pharaohs.

Those who stay within the parish as rebels, who attempt to change the system, to make a case for women from within the church, often find very little support from other women. Perhaps it is unrealistic to expect much support. Moses' passionate act in support of his people, the killing of the Egyptian taskmaster, failed to galvanize the Hebrews. Those who profess contentment with the status quo, or who see no viable alternatives, may actively work against rebellious women, and those with feminist consciousness may have already moved on. Because rebels are perceived by the pastor as meddlesome or threatening, and because they often cannot find a community within the parish, such women, at first fueled by and later drained by their anger, sooner or later may find themselves simply running out of steam.

Reform-minded women who stay "in the church" in order to change it may be in the ironic position of finding their most spiritually enriching support from two groups that are officially defined as "out of the church." The first group has, by its own definition, "left the church." But if "recovering Catholics" are alienated from patriarchal Catholicism, they have not necessarily abandoned their desire for religious community and prayer. Today, many of them are involved in alternative religions, including Goddess worship and witchcraft. In this way, they make ecumenical dialogue a radically different experience and they constitute a potentially rich source of new religious energy. Members of the second group have been defined by Rosemary Ruether as "a community in exodus from patriarchy," though they are perceived by ecclesiastical officials as renegades, heretics, or in some other way effectively "out of the church."[3] Many of this latter group are actively involved in a still undefinable movement known as Womenchurch. Their search for religious alternatives, while genuinely open to insights from nature religions and esoteric religious traditions, also looks to some of the rich heritage of Roman Catholicism. One highly valuable feature of the Womenchurch movement is its refusal to relinquish its place in the church, a refusal that makes a clear distinction between abandoning patriarchy and "leaving the church."

Womenchurch and Traditional Catholicism

Those who perceive themselves as Womenchurch understand that they cannot separate their lives in church from their lives in the world. A politically minded spirituality recognizes that we cannot protect ourselves and our children from reality. Ironically, we also know that we cannot protect the church either: we cannot pretend that it lives in a time and space of its own, unaccountable to the ledgers of social justice. The attempt on the part of Catholic women to redefine themselves as church, while it may be a metaphorical flight to the wilderness, is not a rejection of the tradition. Rather than leaving the church, those involved in the Womenchurch movement are abandoning a model of church life that is no longer persuasive.

Most Catholics grew up in a church that gave us a sense of security. We believed we belonged to the true church. The pre-Vatican II paradigm was classical and conservative: it stressed hierarchical order and control, conceptual permanence, monarchical direction, edict morality, and clear lines of ecclesiastical demarcation. When James Joseph Walsh wrote *The Thirteenth, Greatest of Centuries*, he invoked the pride Catholics had in the old paradigm.[4] Like a number of turn-of-the-century conservatives, his thoroughly romanticized ideal was of a grateful and obedient people ruled over by a wise and benevolent pontiff.

Postconciliar Catholics follow a paradigm that began to emerge in the eighteenth century, the historical, progressive model that shaped much of the work of the Second Vatican Council. It stresses community and communion, developmental symbols, collegial leadership, representative ethics, and ecumenical diversity. I believe we are living in a time when these two paradigms—which we might call hierarchical and equalitarian, or to borrow terminology from the women's movement, patriarchal and feminist—are engaged in a struggle for supremacy. From the patriarchal point of view, women constitute the *last line of defense*: if their position gains support, then the walls of the old system collapse. From the feminist perspective, women's issues are the *last frontier*: our questions open up new worlds for humanity.

The old paradigm supported and was supported by an old deity. The dominant image of God found in the Bible and in the accumulated traditions of the church presided over a hierarchical system in which "He" was the controlling force. Since this God was immutable, almighty, and omniscient, the community formed by "Him" had a great stake in unchanging doctrines, lordly authority, and unquestioning obedience on the part of the faithful. All of these attributes—heavenly and ecclesiastical—were predicated on a belief in absolute truth. The nature of God and the nature of "man" were clear, and the human task was to live according to their laws.

The fundamental question being posed by those whose experience suggests that the divine being might be richer than the sum of "His" patriarchal attributes is simple: what if the nature of God and the nature of humanity is *not* a static given but a progressively created reality? What if God is not "in charge" in the ways many of us have always believed? What if the divine self-communication found in Second-Isaiah, a divine being who suffers with creation, is not meant to describe Jesus but, instead, to describe the God of Jesus? What if God is not all-knowing in the ways we have been taught but is willing and able to respond creatively to genuine novelty? The Indian poet Rabindranath Tagore (1861–1941) said, in one of his mystical reflections, "His own mornings are new surprises to God."

Christian feminist theologians, members of Womenchurch, reform-minded women who continue to stay within the structures of the church, along with feminists who have abandoned formal religion to search for viable women-centered alternatives, are all wandering in the same wilderness. As we look for new sources of spiritual energy, some of us are drawn into the mystical tradition that was born and nurtured among desert dwellers, those called to pray silently in lonely places. Others are searching for the passionate, creation-centered Goddess rejected and abandoned in an ancient desert by a hostile patriarchal priesthood. All of us are trying to find new models of community life, new rituals of celebration, new sources of empowerment, new relationships to the divine, and new rules of conduct.

Feminist Spirituality

Feminist spirituality—a term that often embraces community, ethics, and ritual—is, at its core, a relationship with divinity. On a more personal level, feminist spirituality reflects the search of the woman articulating it. To stay within the framework of my metaphors, I understand myself to be in a wilderness, in exodus from patriarchy. If I find a sense of adventure here, I also know that the desert is a cold, lonely, often frightening place. As someone drawn to the classics of the Catholic mystical tradition, I find that in this new place I have periodic, powerful senses of déjà vu. In this wilderness, where we are called to trust ourselves as well as the re-creative energy of the deity, I see an old God who has promised me things and, at the same time, find that some of my "new" discoveries have probably been hidden here all the time.

Some of those seeking a feminist spirituality spend their time in the wilderness creating new rituals to encompass the full, rich range of human experience and interaction. Others make the connections between spirituality and politics visible and urgent. Still others read and write in an attempt to imagine how everything fits together. We wonder how new understandings of God relate to traditional models, how developing rituals can embody new religious experiences, and how this time in the wilderness might be a locus of new revelation for us all.

I am drawn to alternative theological models and informed by the history of modern theology. Feminist theologians have gained enormously from the work of theological giants like Karl Rahner, whose theory of the supernatural existential makes it possible to consider human experience a fundamental datum for theology. For Rahner, as for many of those searching for a new spirituality, the divine permeation of the human is so intimate and so complete—the divine being is so clearly constitutive of our human existence—that almost everything we say about divinity can be translated into facets of human existence.

The efforts of modern theologians to open the question of revelation so that it is understood in dynamic terms and in contemporary situations of oppression and liberation give feminists a way to claim that their own religious experience might well be a locus for divine self-communication. The work of metaphorical theologians like Sallie McFague, who presents an imaginative picture of God and the world in which God is mother, lover, and friend and the world is God's body, urges all believers to experiment with those metaphors that are most able to interpret the Christian faith powerfully and persuasively for their time.

I am most drawn to process thought, to those theologians and philosophers who see the divine being as creative, responsive love whose power lies in beauty and whose life is involved in the adventure of our own. When I try to imagine an ideal feminist spirituality, certain concepts reappear with regularity. Feminist spirituality must be rooted in and take note of women's collective and individual experience. Sensitive to the connections among all forms of life, it seeks respectful and appreciative coexistence between ourselves and the nonhuman world. Needless to say, it rejects the body/soul dualisms of older forms in favor of more holistic models: the body and its rhythms are as important to us as the hidden world of the psyche. Many have found spiritual insights in the work of contemporary scientists. The notion that all reality is a process of becoming, perishing, and becoming anew has a deep resonance with human experience. Many also believe that there are real clues for spiritual life in the laws of relativity and in the statements about randomness and chance in the work of subatomic physicists.

Because so much of our spiritual past has been destroyed or vitiated by patriarchal fear and hostility, part of any feminist search for spiritual roots requires difficult excavations in dangerous places. We sift through the story of witchcraft and Goddess religion heartbroken at the destruction and energized by our sense of discovery. Since it is possible that great reservoirs of spiritual wisdom might be still hidden, we look for the signs of divine love in unexpected places. Some women feel quite at home in pagan traditions, for example, while others look to the arcane symbols of tarot cards or to the music that seems to come from unconscious memories. Still others try to find space in themselves for other traditions. They may look to the contemplative practices of Eastern religions or to stories of Native American folklore.

In all of these ways, feminists attempting to formulate and practice a new spirituality long for and uphold freedom and seek a divine being who genuinely respects our freedom. Since we have no clear way yet in which to imagine divine activity, we look critically at systems already in place to see what we can learn from them. I think process thought can offer us a great deal. It takes the scientific view of the world seriously, refuses to place human experience outside nature, and believes it essential that every variety of experience be taken into account. Finally, it asks us to give up absolutes, to realize that everything is relative, even the deity.

Process Thought

The God of the patriarchal tradition was explained in Aristotelian categories in opposition to all that is not God. The attributes that defined the divine made God the supreme exception to human experience: we grew and moved, whereas God was perfect and unchangeable, we anguished and changed, whereas God was sublime and complete. It was fairly easy to imagine God having no essential relationship with the world, incapable of being known through modes of human experience. Process thought challenges this traditional notion of an unchanging God.

Process thought is a systematization of the scientific and philosophical work of Alfred North Whitehead (1861–1947), who hoped to explain God in terms of modern experience. Whitehead, an English mathematician turned philosopher, worked on the assumption that all existence, all reality, is continuous: the building blocks of the universe are energy and process, undergoing incessant modification. Process thought, for him, was not a religious construct, but a vision of reality that identified the energy discovered in physics (relativity, chance, randomness, constant movement) with the emotional intensity of human life. Predicated on a modern scientific viewpoint, process thought claims that the universe is not made up of things but of energy. The basic structure of all reality, therefore, is process.[5]

If this assumption seems sensible when applied to human beings or the material world, it may seem inappropriate when applied to God or the spiritual world; yet for Whitehead, God is the supreme example of all metaphysical and human categories, not an exception from them. Since for Whitehead, all existence is continuous, with no breaks, God is part of the process; indeed, God is the ultimate explanation of process. As the metaphysical ground of all process, God is that being who is conditioned and affected by everything that happens everywhere. God is not safely ensconced in some heavenly realm unrelated to our world. On the contrary, God is deeply and necessarily involved in the life of the universe.

If all reality is process and process is defined in terms of relationships, then perfection resides in movement, in ongoing creativity, and relatedness. Since there is no such thing as an isolated process in this system, it makes no sense to speak of God in the abstract, *in se*, to use a scholastic term. God can only be understood in terms of relationships. In this view, God is the most perfectible, most related, and *therefore* most perfect being. Another way to think about divinity is to say that God is full of possibilities, the vision of what might be in the world and in the divine self.

Defining the deity in process terms means beginning with an oxymoron: God is absolutely relative. On the one hand, God is absolute and abstract and has what Whitehead calls the divine primordial nature. On the other hand, the divine being is relative and concrete, having what Whitehead calls the divine consequent nature. The divine primordial nature is the ordered realm of abstract possibilities. Here God is the vision of what might be, embracing all the patterns of all the possible meanings and values relevant to existence. The divine primordial nature, therefore, is God as *possible*, and this side of God's being does not change: it is eternal, present in one timeless vision, the ground of the process. The divine primordial nature cannot be acted upon; it is simply there, or to put it in scholastic terms, God *is*.

The divine primordial nature, however, is totally abstract and has no concrete reality. Since all reality is made up of energy events in constant relationship, this abstract divine vision needs fulfillment in relationship in order to be real. The vision of all possibilities exists only as an abstraction, and for the divine nature to be concrete, to participate in reality, God must experience and relate to all "real things," what Whitehead called "actual concrete occasions." The actualized nature of God, which Whitehead called the divine consequent nature, is *given* by this process. God is actualized by experiencing and relating to all actual concrete occasions. The processes of becoming, which are the real world for us, determine the experience of this divine being. In this sense, God is supremely and absolutely relational and is affected by everything.

The divine consequent nature is thus the divine participation with creatures in the society of being. Why does Whitehead define God in this way? Because, if all reality is process, involving a set of relationships, and if relationships are themselves processes relating to each other in terms of going someplace, then all reality is continually becoming something else, moving to something deeper. The perfection of being is in the movement of the process. It is *in* the becoming, *in* the process as it goes. What is most actual, most real, is that which is most related, in other words, God.

So God is absolute not in the traditional sense of final, total, unlimited, and unchangeable, but in the sense of encompassing in influence, related to, and suffering with all entities and being the ultimate and highest destiny of each. The divine experience is composed of the totality of all experience and is therefore larger and richer than any single actual experience. As single experiences enlarge and increase, which they do as we respond to the divine vision of what might be, God enlarges and increases. The divine experience encompasses, urges, and directs all actual experiences by being at once their fuller context and their most compassionate witness. Since the primary category of existence in this system is "experiencing in process," God is the ever more Becoming One, ever more related, ever more involved.

Furthermore, since the process deity genuinely respects human freedom, God is not coercive. Divine power lies in the lure of beauty, in the tenderness of compassionate persuasion, not in force. In the old system, God was the total, efficient cause of all things, able to produce anything, to create out of nothing. But in this sytem, the process contains its own inner dynamic. God has the vision of all possibilities and is the source of all value, but God has no power of coercion toward the actualization of this value.

God has only the power of what Whitehead calls "suasion." The divine vision of the best possible interrelationships presents an aim to the process and functions as a lure to it, but cannot compel it. God shares the power of being with creatures and allows all of us freedom and spontaneity. The divine/human interaction, therefore, is a real history of intercommunication. We need God's primordial nature (the vision of all possibilities), and God's consequent nature needs our choices and experience in order to become actualized and real. In this way, everything that happens makes a difference to God because God has to respond to it and take it into the divine life, adjust it within the harmony of the divine plan.

What remains fixed for God is the absolute integrity of the divine aim that looks toward the fullness of life for all creation. But to move toward this fulfillment, God shares in the concreteness of events. Every achievement of good, of value, of meaning in the world increases the richness of God's being. God is not the world process, but God is *in* the process, is the eternal structure and power that makes the world possible and that participates in each moment of the world's becoming, for the world is nothing without God.

As Daniel Day Williams says, "Process philosophy opens up for Christian theology a way of conceiving the being of God in historical-temporal terms. What it proposes is akin to the existentialist search for radical freedom for [hu]man[ity] and acceptance of the risks of being."[6] In the biblical sense, God works in time and history where people can refuse initiatives, overturn the most wonderful plans, and divert the most clearly articulated divine aims. Yet the God of the Bible continually re-creates good possibilities for those same people. God as understood in process thought is creative love that is persuasive, responsive, and involved. The divine being in the biblical wilderness, who joins a wandering people with a sense of adventure, who works and acts within the limitations given by the actual situation, and who longs for things to go well but is willing to present new opportunities when they do not, is very much a process God.

In terms of the feminist critique of Catholicism, whether we are in exodus from patriarchy or alienated and exiled from our religious tradition, we wander with a certain set of limitations and are lured on by visions of new possibilities. Like Yahweh, who promised a land of milk and honey, God—understood by many feminist interpreters as Goddess—presents new visions to us and entices us toward their fulfillment. And like the biblical deity, this one is willing to adjust to our weakness or blindness or fatigue along the way, and to stay with us on the journey.

Wandering in the wilderness is not lightly undertaken. It is a perilous journey on which we are searching for new language, new ways of understanding human interaction, new spiritual frameworks that contain political imperatives, and new ways of celebrating who we are in relation to the divine being and to the universe. The interactive aspects of the biblical God interpreted through process thought suggest that those in exile from patriarchy are accompanied in the wilderness by a divine being who has visions of our best possibilities yet is willing to suffer with our defeats. Because God must work within human limitations, things might not always work out the way God envisions them. Because our lives in the wilderness determine the divine destiny along with our own, we are in radical partnership with a deity willing to take risks.

Religious experience has claimed that human beings relate to God in strength, love, vulnerability, and weakness. Process thought makes the same claims for the divine being. God relates to us in strength because of the vision present in the divine primordial nature, in love because of a desire for more extensive and intensive relationship, in vulnerability because the divine destiny is tied to ours, and in weakness because God needs what we can give. Put another way, I would say that God holds on to nothing. Because of process, God lets go of everything all the time. Everything dies and becomes new at every moment with God. In the process God, there is a sense of struggle that can support those whose religious lives are struggles.

Feminist Harmonies in Process Spirituality

The original desert of the exodus experience was a place of testing, as the desert of the Isaian reinterpretation was a location of nurturance. The wilderness many feminists find themselves in at the moment can be both: through suffering and solace we may be in a unique position to come to a deeper awareness of the kind of deity we long for when we reject the limited God of the patriarchy. In the present wilderness, feminists nurture and test one another as we search for and relate to a divine being of genuine mutuality. One might even say that the wilderness experience, the contemporary search for a feminist spirituality, is another way to understand covenant.

The Israelites experienced God through the covenant, a promise of relationship that carried a profound commitment to love and be present to one another forever. Yahweh's words, "I will be your God and you will be my people," are a promise to abide with and interact with that people. As Margaret Farley reminds us, we know from biblical history that the Jews fixed upon different aspects of the divine promise at different moments in their lives. The covenant was identified with land and progeny with Abraham; with liberation and refuge in the Mosaic period; with peace and order in the kingdom of David; with wisdom and justice in the prophetic traditions; and after the exile, with the promise of a new kingdom of some sort.[7] Throughout these developments, however, we can find some constants. The divine promise is one of ongoing love; it depends in part on choices, as Yahweh's upholding of the covenant depended upon Israel's holding to its stipulations; it sustains life in the present moment; and it draws people toward a future realm of justice.

In the original exodus story, the biblical author focuses on Moses, the Red Sea miracle, the giving of the law at Sinai, and other important events. Almost as an aside, the author notes (Exod. 15:20) that Miriam, the prophetess, the sister of Moses and Aaron, took a timbrel in her hand, and all the women went out after her and danced. Music is an important part of new feminist spirituality. Songs have become metaphors for our journeys, ways to achieve solidarity, sustaining rhythms, and empowering chants. Dance, too, is a special part of our spirituality, and like the poets who saw the cosmic dance as encompassing and circular, feminists like to believe that we are "dancing Sarah's circle" rather than "climbing Jacob's ladder."

Marjorie Suchocki, in trying to describe the mysterious, intimate, joyful, related, triune reality of the process God, says that we must turn to metaphor and imagination to express that reality. Her analog for the process God is that of a special, even fantastic symphony. Imagine a symphony, she writes, in which each note is intensely alive. Each note feels itself in relation to all the others, feels its place in the whole, and feels the whole as well. The life that sustains the lives of the notes is the symphony as a whole. On a deeper level of awareness, suppose we say that the symphony as a whole is alive, a living symphony sparkling with awareness of its own beauty, both from the perspective of the whole and from the multiplied perspectives of each part. The single beauty is intensified through the multiple awarenesses merged into the unified awareness of the whole. Now, imagine someone outside that symphony appreciatively attuned to its complex beauty. Imagine that every listener becomes a participant in the symphony, adding a new note, and that the symphony is ever deepening, ever intensifying, infinitely beautiful, and that it lasts forever.[8]

If this metaphor gives some notion of the process God, then perhaps Miriam and the women were the only ones who really heard the deeper possibilities of the first exodus. Perhaps Second-Isaiah was profoundly insightful telling the Jews to "sing a new song" and enter the new Jerusalem dancing. Miriam and Second-Isaiah saw, perhaps, what feminists attempt to see when searching for a genuinely feminist spirituality, that the Holy One wants our enjoyment of life's possibilities to be contagious, to increase the enjoyment of others, and to lead to a new understanding of the divine being in covenant with us.

Conclusion

In redefining the wilderness, my concern is not with being lost in the middle of a desert, but with what or who might be encountered in that place. The process God, a minor theme of the Christian tradition, has always been there. Some of the mystics have known it. Some of the poets have celebrated its sensuousness and ability to captivate the heart. Tagore sings eloquently of the pleasures of divine love in ways that feminist pilgrims might find attractive. "Deliverance is not for me in renunciation," he muses, talking to the divine being, "I feel the embrace of freedom in a thousand bonds of delight . . . I will never shut the door of my senses. The delights of sight and hearing and touch will bear thy delight."[9] His poetry is redolent with images of song, and of ways to find interactive pleasure with a deity who longs for our joy as well as our company, who says, in effect, "You can sit mourning by the waters of Babylon forever, or you can compose a new song, a song with your own good parts of the past remembered in it."

Whether feminists relate more directly to the original Hebrews or to the postexilic Jews of the Isaian tradition, we can find some joy in our wilderness. Those who sense new life in the search for a feminist spirituality compose and sing new songs. Those who have left the land of the Pharaohs only to find themselves in an environment with new terrors and profound loneliness may not be inclined to take up their timbrels and dance. The only certainty at this point is that we cannot return to patriarchal religion. At the same time, many of us refuse to be read out of our heritage, and so we seek the harmonies of its minor themes and look for ways to relate to its life-giving aspects.

In this new territory, this wilderness of loneliness and desire, I believe we can find what has been there all along, waiting for discovery: a divine being infinitely richer than anything imagined by the patriarchs; containing a fullness of nature that makes sense of the divine image as male *and* female; passionately involved with our lives, eager for our enjoyment, supportive of our adventures, full of new possibilities, and thus, with us, hopeful about the future.

WHO IS THE GODDESS AND WHERE DOES SHE GET US?

Neopaganism and Utopian

Poetics

This essay was inspired by my students at Indiana University. In 1985 I taught a new course on the "feminist critique of Western religion," which drew students from all parts of the university. Members of the class were a mixed lot: some of them had no idea why women would want to criticize religion, and others had left patriarchal religion behind while they were in high school; some of them were expecting a defense of religion against the complaints of feminists, and others hoping for a diatribe against women who still believed in God the Father. I had designed the course as an introductory survey to stimulate discussion about problems some women had with sexist language in biblical and liturgical texts, complementarity, ordination, the God-symbol, and other such issues.

In a half-hearted attempt to broaden the course, I included a unit on Goddess spirituality. To say that I was not keen on the Goddess puts it mildly. Part of my uneasiness stemmed from a bias about the adequacy of the sources on which this religious expression was constructed. I was also frustrated by the tendency of the women's movement to connect feminist spirituality exclusively to Goddess worship and witchcraft. Nearly all of the books, workshops, and conferences on feminist spirituality that I heard about were devoted to explorations of the roots of modern witchcraft or of neopaganism, featuring Goddess ritual. Since the religious lives of most women have been shaped by *different religious traditions, I saw no reason to restrict the discussion of feminist spirituality to what seemed to me a fictive and romantic outlook.*

My frustration with Goddess religion manifested itself in class as active skepticism. My introduction of Goddess spirituality did not take it seriously as a religious alternative, and I was ready to give it a very quick reading. My best student and a few others were clearly agitated by this treatment. They complained vociferously about what I was doing, and it took me a few minutes to realize that they were defending a belief system of their own. I do not know why I had imagined that no one who worshiped the Goddess would ever appear in my classes. Their presence surprised me. But the students were quite right to protest my lack of sympathy. Astonished by their anguish and impressed with their passion, I resolved to treat neopaganism with the same kind of reverent attention I brought to any other spiritual reality.

As I read more about Goddess religion and talked with my students inside and outside the classroom, I had an idea for a conference. With the help of the women's studies program, Indiana University sponsored a series of events—papers, exhibits, panel discussions, happenings—called "Neopaganism: A Feminist Search for Religious Alternatives." I opened the series with this essay, an attempt to survey the territory and to find the best possible light in which to view Goddess religion. The highlight of that series was a talk—probably better described as a guided experience—by Starhawk, one of the best-known and most articulate witches in America. All in all, we managed to bring a different perception of religious experience to campus, and to attract members of the local community who, I imagine, had had very little to do with the university before. Witches, warlocks, members of a local elfin community, members of local feminist collectives, and other nontraditional students of religion turned out.

My essay, building on my sense of obligation to my students and to myself, does not explain the rituals and possibilities of Goddess religion so much as it sets the questions in a historical and interpretive context. I have attempted to make sense of a phenomenon that many scholars, myself included, have been quick to dismiss. I also wanted to show that the way one constructs a religious explanation of the universe is probably based upon differences in religious autobiography and need not have a historical foundation. As a religious studies professional, I believe strongly that true religious experience is available to all people and is mediated through a wide variety of expressions in the cultures of the world. It was important for me to be able to perceive neopaganism in this light.

Although I am not personally drawn to Goddess religion or witchcraft, many of the themes that I have used to urge Catholic feminists to find new territory for themselves within their church could just as well be used by those whose religious experience centers on the Goddess. They, too, have stories of pain and rage, have felt themselves called to a new land, and have entered into the desert on a determined search for new manifestations of the deity.

As I gathered material for this essay, I tried to conjure up a vision of some of the nineteenth-century leaders of the women's movement "casting a circle" or "drawing down the moon." Negative associations were easy enough to imagine: I could hear hostile male critics calling Susan B. Anthony a "witch," for example, and referring to the radical Matilda Joslyn Gage as "demonic." Such words have often been used to discredit and threaten strong single women who operate in defiance of patriarchal norms. Positive connections were harder to come by: the idea of maternal Elizabeth Cady Stanton dancing at a moonlit solstice celebration made me collapse with laughter. Although this failure of imagination says more about me than it does about witchcraft, I must still insist that nineteenth-century feminist leaders do not guide me to the *practices* of neopaganism. Nevertheless, I am convinced that their iconoclastic religious writings helped to make the current revival of Goddess religion possible. Stanton and Gage particularly, in urging women to reject the authority of the Bible and the institutional church, raise a challenge that, although ignored or condemned in their own time, has been taken up by neopagan feminists.[1]

Emergence of Neopaganism in the 1970s

Neopaganism is a generic term for a loosely connected group of practitioners who believe that their religious tradition is older than any of the major world religions. Neopaganism includes contemporary revivals of witchcraft and Goddess religion as well as Druids, believers in old Celtic religion, and others. Marked by eclecticism, neopaganism has emotional or psychic bonds with many other religious and quasi-religious groups. I am most interested in the revival of Goddess religion by a significant number of American feminists, and I mention witchcraft because it has been defined by some as a Goddess religion.

Although my title asks where the Goddess "gets us," I might just as well have asked where we "get her," since the arguments over historical evidence have been particularly acrimonious and belabored. At the same time, I think it can be shown that questions surrounding the revival of Goddess religion can provide a different perspective on some important feminist concerns. As a religious studies scholar, I am especially interested in the ways in which the claims of Goddess religionists raise questions about history, authority, and language. Furthermore, when I interpret feminist spirituality as a quest, I can see some of the ways in which neopaganism functions as a utopian poetics, drawing believers into a better future.

What does it mean to talk about or believe in "the Goddess" when the evidence for her existence is entirely preliterate? What connection is there between the absence of written texts and the disdain for dogma in neopaganism? Is it easier, in other words, to imagine an equalitarian religion when one can surmise its tenets rather than having to extract them from ancient texts? What kind of authority can a misogynist tradition claim over women? Does the rejection of biblical and ecclesiastical authority as recommended by Stanton and Gage necessarily lead to a rejection of religion, or can it lead to the creation of a new one? Finally, when neopagan practitioners appear satisfied with the Goddess as a psychic reality, must we conclude that they cannot find objective verification for her existence or that they do not need it? And if they do not need it, then how does Goddess religion function mythically within the human community? I will raise some of these questions in a broad context in the hope that the intellectual issues embedded in the rise of neopaganism will not be obscured by the emotional field surrounding them. In order to produce the *status questionae*, however, I need to set this highly complex phenomenon of neopaganism into a manageable historical context.

Although there were earlier contributions to the debate, for example, Z. Budapest's *The Feminist Book of Light and Shadows*, let me choose Halloween 1979 as my starting point.[2] This date is memorable for the publication of two major works on witchcraft and Goddess religion: Margot Adler covered the East Coast with her comprehensive study of neopaganism, *Drawing Down the Moon*, while Starhawk represented the West Coast with *The Spiral Dance*, her handbook of witchcraft as Goddess religion.[3] Under the light of a not quite full October moon, from coast to coast, American feminists were invited to consider a viable religious alternative, a new religion claiming to be a revival of the Old Religion.

By 1979, the feminist search for religious alternatives was not news. Discouraged by a textual heritage that appeared to deny women's experience, some scholars were attempting to discover and integrate feminine dimensions of the divine into the mainstreams of the tradition. Others believed that "the Goddess" was the only proper guide to a new religious world. With the publication of *Gyn/Ecology* (1978) Mary Daly, one of the most original feminist theologians, severed all links with patriarchal religion in general and Christianity in particular. Arguing that men were naturally necrophilic, their religions inexorably patriarchal, and their world on the verge of disaster, she made a case for Goddess religion as a separatist search for creative transcendence and urged women to reclaim their biophilic natures. If Rosemary Ruether, a prolific, but more moderate critic of conventional Christianity, was still involved in the bracing project of recovery, she had also published a collection of essays that linked theological revolution with ecology and with nonbiblical religion.[4]

By 1979 old icons like Mary, the mother of Jesus, appeared to have no place in the women's movement. Indeed, in a sweeping historical analysis, Marina Warner had shown that there could be no solace in a figure that had been so thoroughly coopted by the patriarchs and used effectively for so long to relegate women to subservient positions.[5] Later attempts to reclaim Mary, including my own, tried to emphasize her independence and majesty, attributes of mythical goddesses in poetry and world religions, but the energy of the moment was with "real" Goddess figures, not with Christian saints who, whatever their attributes, functioned to support the institutional church.[6]

The enthusiasm of feminist theologians for Goddess religion can be linked to the work of an art historian and sculptor, Merlin Stone. Her provocative *When God Was a Woman* (1976) quickly became a mainstay for those who were unable to abandon religion altogether, but equally unable to participate in what they considered to be religious traditions that were fundamentally harmful to women. Taking a popular biblical metaphor, we might say that whereas Mary Daly had engineered the exodus event (when she led women out of the Harvard Divinity School chapel in 1972, consciously using the exodus story as her theme), Merlin Stone led them to the promised land. She encouraged women to experience God in female terms and, later, to connect that experience with what she called the "ancient mirrors of womanhood," Goddess and heroine lore from around the world.[7]

In the closing days of the 1970s, thoroughly discontented with their own traditions, a group of feminist theologians and historians began their pursuit of Goddess religion as a realistic alternative to Judaism and Christianity. Stone's work, although not above serious criticism, was enormously influential.[8] In many ways, it called for and supported a revolution. The energy of Stone's appeal was translated into a scholarly argument by Carol P. Christ, who continues to be one of the primary supporters of Goddess religion as an alternative to Judaism and Christianity.

Building on a provocative distinction originally suggested by Sheila D. Collins, Christ published a review of feminist theological literature in the fall of 1977 that categorized feminist theologians either as "reformist" or "revolutionary" on the basis of their response to Mary Daly's work. "A serious Christian response to Daly's criticism," argued Christ, "either will have to show that the . . . symbolism of Father and Son [does] not have the effect of reinforcing and legitimating male power and female submission, or it will have to transform Christian imagery at its very core."⁹ To Christ's way of thinking, Rosemary Ruether and others whose work concentrated on revisionary readings of the tradition were swimming against the current: reform would be impossible in a totally intractable patriarchal institution. Revolutionaries, on the other hand, urged women to search through history and prehistory to find new myths of female empowerment. Penelope Washbourn, for example, supported revolution because she created new rituals that used women's experiences as a starting point for theology. Stories of goddesses and matriarchies were considered crucial to a revolutionary consciousness and Christ's own work with Judith Plaskow, *Womanspirit Rising* (1979), won wide popular support partly because its argument culminated in the claim that "women need the Goddess."[10]

At the heart of the revolutionary project, Christ argued both in her review article and in *Womanspirit Rising*, is the rejection of the authority of Scripture and organized religion, an echo of Stanton and Gage that would often be heard by feminist theologians in the coming years. The rejection of traditional religious authority in favor of a total reliance on women's experience had a growing community of support by 1979. Naomi Goldenberg's *Changing of the Gods* (1979) offered a "phenomenology of modern witchcraft" and set the revival of Goddess worship in the context of a female quest for power, noting that all legitimate power for women is based on the great pagan goddesses of the ancient world. Goldenberg urged women to trust their subconscious and to listen to their dreams, both of which would be more religiously useful to them than patriarchal texts and practices. Elaine Pagels, who won the National Book Award with *The Gnostic Gospels* (1979), suggested that controversies in the early Christian movement might be read today for their insight into the pluriform possibilities of ancient Christianity. Women were thus not limited to their own primary experiences. Indeed, they could trust ancient Christian history, could find venerable texts showing that it was possible, within the parameters of Christianity, to imagine a Mother God and to focus on immediate experience, ecstasy, and divinization.[11]

As we moved into the 1980s, excitement about "the Goddess" and expansion of "the Craft" seemed to reach everywhere. Since one of the tenets of the women's movement demands as full a representation of women's ideas and practices as possible, meetings related to what many began to call "womanspirit" were enormously varied. Conferences attracted scholars, practicing witches, pantheists, healers, tarot readers, repertory groups devoted to staging Goddess events, and a host of other women's groups that were drawn to what Charlene Spretnak called "the rise of spiritual power within the feminist movement."[12] By the mid-1980s, "feminist spirituality" had come to mean that set of religious experiences clustered around Goddess religion and witchcraft. Stories about housewives in Ohio offering the fruits of the harvest to Isis in a civic festival were as much a part of this new movement as bibliographies on Goddess religion published by women's studies programs and seminary consortiums. Even *Women's Sports and Fitness* ran a story on South Pacific island women who juggle, claiming that men cannot do it with the same skill because their efforts are not blessed by an ancient Goddess of the underworld.

Rosemary Ruether and Carol Christ: Two Views of Goddess Religion

If the energy of Goddess religion and the rise of modern witchcraft gave a thrill of excitement to the field of feminist theology, they also presented it with enormous problems. Christ's division of feminist theologians into (mere) reformers and (marvelous) revolutionaries caused some stir of its own as various writers attempted refinements of the distinction or denied its validity altogether. At the same time, the claims of Goddess feminists and witches raised vexing questions of definition, historical verifiability, the nature of religious evidence, and the authority of biblical religion. Most important, Christ's challenge sparked a debate that appeared to call for feminists to choose sides: it presented the issue of whether one works within a tradition or outside of it as an argument to be settled by reason and implied that abandonment of particular traditions was the most logical conclusion. In order to bring a cluster of debatable issues into focus and to interrogate the challenge itself, I use the work of Christ, a revolutionary, and of Ruether, a radical reformer. Their work is pertinent not only because they represent two different perspectives, but because they have been involved in a public debate about Goddess religion since 1979.

Although Ruether had written about witchcraft in a 1975 essay, she did not begin to raise serious questions about Goddess religion until 1979, the year of *The Spiral Dance*, *The Changing of the Gods*, and *Gyn/Ecology*. Ruether's own agenda is based on a radical reading of the prophetic tradition, and she criticized "that branch of the feminist spirituality movement that has rejected biblical religion and turned to the alternative religion of the Goddess."[13] Her questions appear to be straightforward—for example, on what basis do Goddess feminists totally reject the Bible, and how helpful is the specific alternative they offer?—but they are rooted in her belief that real feminists are radical revisionaries working within some religious tradition. The key to an authentic feminist critique of culture, she believes, is the discovery of the liberating potential of an authoritative tradition.[14] Goddess feminists, according to Ruether, are narrow-minded in their reading of the Bible, bigoted in their separatism, and simply wrong about the historical background of "the Great Goddess." Drawing on her training in classics, Ruether argued that ancient Goddess religion did not valorize women or give them special privileges in their societies; on the contrary, Goddess religions existed to glorify male power over women.

Christ's response to Ruether, much like her 1977 review essay, focused on the absolutely crucial nature of the male God symbol in Judaism and Christianity. The contemporary oppression of women, she believes, is a logical outcome of the core symbolism of God/He. That being the case, the "patriarchal attitudes of the majority of those whose religious faith is based on the Bible will not be changed until the image of God is changed."[15] In response to Ruether's use of biblical prophets as a critical norm, Christ insisted that the prophetic tradition is at the root of religious intolerance: "I do not believe the prophetic-messianic tradition can function as a basis for feminist theology."[16] Again, the arguments appear to be straight-forward, but they are imbedded in her belief that real feminists are revolutionaries who reject the biblical tradition in favor of a journey to the Goddess.

Judging from a hastily re-formed session at the National Women's Studies Association meeting in June 1980, Ruether's article shocked and wounded Christ and Goldenberg, who took the opportunity to "answer" Ruether publicly and without much warning. That session, and the proliferation of Goddess events, meetings, and publications, led to Ruether's second article, "Goddess and Witches: Liberation and Countercultural Feminism," published in September 1980. Arguing that the creation of a feminist spirituality "needs synthesis and transformation, not separation and rejection," she criticized Goddess feminists for the absence or misuse of historical evidence; for articulating a simple-minded anthropology in which males are necrophilic whereas females are biophilic; for writing what amounted to escapist fiction; and for reducing complex theological questions like immanence and transcendence to a male/female dichotomy.[17]

Although the direct responses to Ruether were confined to a few letters to the editor, the debate raged on at national meetings, at conferences—for example, the Womenspirit Bonding conference at Grailville in July 1982—and at the separate celebratory events of neopagans and Womenchurch feminists. Furthermore, it continues to provide a significant dialectical moment not only for the women's movement, but as Goddess feminists have claimed all along, for the future of the planet.

Evidence for and against the Goddess

It is worth pausing a moment to consider the substance of the Ruether/Christ debate since it turns on issues that vex feminist critics in other disciplines, namely those of historical evidence and reconstruction, canonical authority and written texts, androcentric symbols and language.

One of the main arguments against Goddess religion and witch-craft centers on the lack of clear historical evidence for their claims. Scholars have been quick to point to the flimsy if not altogether nonexistent evidence for primal matriarchies or for a religion devoted to "the Great Goddess." Two different issues are at stake here: the existence of matriarchies in the ancient world, and the existence of a single Great Goddess worshiped in such a world. The matriarchal issue is the one that has received the most negative response from scholars, and it may be something of a red herring. Margot Adler notes that it is fashionable for scholars to dismiss the idea, and Charlene Spretnak claims that the rejection of matriarchy by feminist scholars on historical grounds obscures deeper issues of meaning. Whether one can locate a real matriarchal society is not so important to Spretnak as whether the *concept* of woman was different in ancient Goddess-centered societies than in patriarchal ones.

The first level of response from Goddess practitioners, captured in the poignant words of poet Adrienne Rich, was sadness: "My heart is moved by all I cannot save/so much has been destroyed."[18] That sadness soon changed to anger and blame: it was the patriarchs who destroyed the records, burned the women, and set humanity on a collision course with self-destruction, said Mary Daly in *Gyn/Ecology*, and other Goddess feminists repeated it. When critics complained that the explanation itself was mythic, predicated on a nonexistent primal matriarchy, the response was more clearly designed to prove neopagan claims using scholarly sources. Excavations by British archaeologist James Mellaart and by University of California archaeologist Marija Gimbutas were used to supplement the claims of Merlin Stone, and the argument moved from the absence of sources to the nature of the evidence.

The problems are rooted in the fact that there is no written evidence for the existence of primal matriarchies or the Great Goddess: all the "proof" as adduced by scholars and their interpreters is based on Neolithic cave paintings and prehistoric pottery remains. Textual evidence about goddesses comes from male poets and historians like Homer and Hesiod and, while useful for describing attributes of Greek goddesses, it cannot be extrapolated to draw conclusions either about the lives of women in ancient cultures or about prehistoric precursors of those goddesses. The contemporary penchant for understanding witchcraft as an ancient, universal matriarchal tradition practiced in secret underground societies throughout human history—for example, as presented by British folklorist Margaret Murray—has been dismissed by scholars. Finally, some of the feminist scholars who write passionately about prehistoric Goddess religion and ancient powers of women are themselves not trained in the scholarly tools of ancient history or archaeology. Judith Ochshorn's *Female Experience and the Nature of the Divine*, for example, has been criticized both by scholars of the ancient Near East and by other feminists for its reliance on secondary and sometimes untrustworthy literature and for its overstated conclusions.[19]

In the face of this kind of questioning, Goddess feminists and witches have adopted several different responses. Merlin Stone, to whom the prehistoric evidence is clear, refuses to argue about it any more. Naomi Goldenberg, whose interests are more clearly Jungian, chooses to ignore historical problems in favor of the psychic reality Goddess religion has for its adherents. Others, in repeating the refrain about lost sources, implicitly raise questions about what kinds of evidence one can use.

Feminist historians have learned to extract a good deal of information from inscriptions, myths, drawings, and other obscure places; they have found ways to get behind a given text in order to discover what has been omitted from it. Feminist theologians, however, in an attempt to reconstruct religious history, must first choose a norm, that is to say, an evaluating device with which to make judgments and sift evidence. Those called "reformers" by Christ find their critical norm within the text or the tradition. Ruether, for example, uses the prophetic cry for justice (as found in the Bible) as a means to reject oppressive biblical texts. Measured against prophetic messianism, says Ruether, those texts that demean women are blasphemous. Clearly, however, a textually devised norm, whatever its radical capabilities, will not help "revolutionaries": Goddess feminists reject the texts as a first step toward creating a new religion from prehistorical sources and contemporary female experience.

At the same time, Goddess theologians like Christ and Christine Downing appear to long for historical verification: they clearly want to link contemporary Goddess religion to ancient textual evidence to show that this "new religion" is, in some respects, a revival of an old one. If the ancient written sources are androcentric, however, how can they be used by feminists? Is there an interpretive principle imbedded within the texts themselves, or do Goddess scholars need an extrinsic evaluative norm?

A New Feminist Hermeneutic

At this juncture, it is useful to turn to Elisabeth Schüssler Fiorenza, a New Testament critic who works from within the Christian tradition but who nevertheless uses a norm not derived from the text as her critical principle. In her powerful book *In Memory of Her* (1983), she argues that women's past and present experience is the only standard a radical feminist hermeneutics can use. Carol Christ has recently turned to Schüssler Fiorenza as a methodological guide in her attempt to reconstruct the mythic past faithfully. For Schüssler Fiorenza, and now for Christ, "feminist critical method [can] be likened to the work of a detective in that it does not rely solely on historical 'facts' nor invent its evidence but is engaged in an imaginative reconstruction of reality."[20]

Because it is in many ways indebted to liberation theology, Schüssler Fiorenza's method is clearly political and modern, but it is also reminiscent of the work of nineteenth-century feminists, especially on the issue of canonical authority. In *The Woman's Bible*, Elizabeth Cady Stanton argued that the Bible was a political weapon used by men against women, and that it was written by men not by God. The authority of the Bible therefore ought to be questioned, and the texts ought to be weighed and interpreted in the light of some critical principle. Stanton's critical principle appears to have been a combination of common sense and new translations of troublesome passages. Schüssler Fiorenza, using Stanton as a starting point, makes the experience of women her measuring rod.

Whatever the merits of Schüssler Fiorenza's hermeneutics in New Testament circles, her willingness to "read the silences" and to be continually suspicious of "androcentric texts" makes her an attractive guide for Goddess feminists. If Schüssler Fiorenza's hermeneutical principle is adapted by Goddess feminists, it might enable them to read androcentric texts about ancient goddesses, measure them against women's experiences—ancient and modern—and then attempt a reconstruction of the origins of Goddess religion. Whether such a project is feasible I do not know, but it appears to me that it is worth considering since it allows neopagan scholars to use and evaluate the written evidence that has heretofore been used against them.

A reconstructive or reimaginative method allows interpreters to choose certain aspects of ancient goddesses and reject others. Christ, for example, rejects the goddess Athena because of her association with war: "I judge everything I learn from the past on the basis of my own experience as shaped, named and confirmed by the voices of my sisters."[21] She can do that partly because Goddess traditions are not normative for her in the way that Scripture is normative for Christians, but also because the principle of women's experience, as named and confirmed in community, is her winnowing fan.

Once the possibility of choosing one's own religious symbols is introduced into the argument, I find myself back to the opening challenge in this debate: feminist theologians either have to show that the core symbolism of Christianity is not hopelessly sexist or they have to abandon it in search of a new religion. Ruether and others have said repeatedly that the male God-language of Judaism and Christianity is harmful for women, and that the practices of the Christian church have been odious where women are concerned. Ruether admits that the witch craze is a harvest of the Christian traditions of misogyny and sexual repression, and she clearly recognizes that contemporary policy in the churches is bad for women. Nevertheless, she says, the tradition can and must be subverted from the inside. The critical principles must be derived from the tradition itself. Ruether's position has strong support from like-minded feminist theologians. Anne Carr, for example, in her feminist theological reconstruction *Transforming Grace* (1988), uses modern philosophical theology to reinterpret Christian symbols. She bases her conclusions on the nature of symbols themselves, arguing that they possess a drive toward a transcendence of their own culture-bound formulations. Religious symbols may be oppressive, in other words, but they are also something more than oppressive. Since all religious symbols can move beyond the social and political patterns they have legitimated, it is imperative that religious feminists not abandon their religious traditions without attempting to reformulate the great symbol systems of those traditions for themselves.[22]

Carr and other theologians understand the theological task as the accommodation of an eternally valid revelation to the temporal and cultural uncertainties of symbol and gesture as they are expressed in the changing language, experience, and sensibility of human societies over time. Sallie McFague makes a modern attempt to lift the veil of language and culture in *Models of God: Theology for an Ecological, Nuclear Age* (1987). She argues that all theology is metaphorical construction and that each age must experiment with those metaphors most able to interpret beliefs persuasively for its own time.[23]

One way to approach Goddess spirituality, therefore, is through a theological reinterpretation of the tradition. One notices the limitations in the texts and practices of Christianity and seeks ways to expand religious expression so that it includes the experience of women. Since all theological language is inadequate by definition, it is possible to reimagine the core symbolism of Christianity in new metaphors. Since liturgical practice has been unfairly limited to male perception and privilege, it is possible to redesign religious celebration so that it is more clearly representative of and responsive to the community. All of these approaches build on the tradition and are predicated on the belief that it is worth saving.

Christ, on the other hand, and those who share her views, find the core symbolism of Christianity hopeless. For Goddess feminists, rejection of the authority of Scripture and tradition are presuppositions, and the task of feminist theology is to create new symbols rather than to reinterpret traditional ones. "Out of our intuition, experience, and research," Christ says, "some of us are creating Goddess traditions anew."[24] Like many feminists who have rejected religion altogether, Christ believes that efforts to reinterpret the misogynist statements of the Bible, the Qur'an, or the Talmud bog down in their own casuistry. The only alternative for her is a search for female symbolism outside the tradition, which can then be introduced alongside male symbols so that the Deity can be fully represented in dual imagery.

The arguments between Christ and Ruether appear to lead to an impasse, because they are rooted in a strategic choice: does a feminist with religious predilections work best within a given tradition or apart from it? Are feminists today confronted with the choice Elijah gave the ancient Hebrews: "Choose this day whom you will serve"? Such a dramatic demand seems to surround the discussion of Goddess religion, but I suspect that the choice is unnecessary. If Goddess feminists and traditional religious feminists share a general respect for religion in human life, if they both understand the need for community, and if they both long for some ritual reenactments of a central religious vision, then perhaps the division of their two camps is not as deep as it seems.

For centuries Christianity has grounded its claims to truthfulness on the historical facts of the life and work of Jesus. Contrary to those religions whose origins are hidden in the misty, prehistoric past, Christianity claims to have encountered God in the historical events surrounding a verifiable historical figure. I do not want to suggest that questions of "truth" are not important in religion, but I believe that a traditional religious approach to truth as historically verifiable may be more appealing to some than to others. Neopaganism offers a religious alternative that rests on a utopian vision rather than a historical one, and our attempt to understand it should be sympathetic to the differences.

Goddess feminists do not reject religion, nor do they despise symbols. On the contrary, Christ argues that people need to be open to the mysterious dimension of life and concludes that life is diminished without symbols. Her theological point is simple: God is a symbol that may no longer serve us, whereas Goddess has within it liberating principles both for women and for humanity. What I find radical about Goddess feminists is not the rejection of God, but the determination to live a life rich in religious experience, ritual, and community. Goddess feminists are thus engaged in a triangulated dialogue within religious studies. One group—including revisionary feminist theologians—hopes to reinterpret Christian symbols. Another, not necessarily involved in feminist questions at all and represented by Harvard theologian Gordon Kaufman, advises getting rid of symbols altogether.[25] Finally, Goddess feminists insist on their right to create new symbolic expressions of feminist religious consciousness. At its best, this lively and radically ecumenical discussion can reflect an existential pluralism.

Goddess Spirituality and Utopian Poetics

If Goddess feminism is perceived as a quest motivated by religious experience, then it has a right to be valued as authentic, at least *as a religious experience*. I am reminded of William James's musings about mysticism, an experience he did not find credible. Yet as a psychologist of religion who spent many years observing spiritual phenomena and human behavior, he was unwilling to reject its power to open believers to new dimensions of religious experience. After gathering massive evidence about mystical states in a variety of the world's religions, he concluded that mystics "tell of the supremacy of the ideal, of vastness, of union, of safety, and of rest. They offer us *hypotheses*, hypotheses which we may voluntarily ignore, but which as thinkers we cannot possibly upset. The supernaturalism and optimism to which they would persuade us may, interpreted in one way or another, be after all the truest of insights into the meaning of this life."[26]

Following the general suggestions offered by James, I think we can find it useful to imagine Goddess feminism offering hypotheses that might upset our traditional notions of religion. What might those hypotheses be? We have already noted that Goddess feminists have a new approach to questions of text and canonicity. We have seen, too, that their reliance on women's experience, though generally no different from the experiential base of most feminist discourse, is much more radical. Like many religious groups, Goddess feminists also participate to some extent in political activism.

One of the criticisms against Goddess religion—leveled both by theologians and by feminists whose work demands certain political commitments—has been that it is romantic, solipsistic, and politically lethargic. It is not clear to me, however, that Goddess religion has any greater share of dreamy idealists within it than any other religion. Indeed, those feminists who speak for Goddess religion extol the value of political action and tend to be significantly involved in a variety of grass roots movements. The political goals of those Goddess feminists represented by Starhawk's *Truth or Dare* (1988), for example, are rooted in the hope for a better humanity.[27] In this way, neopaganism is connected to the general lines of the humanist agenda: the hope for peace, for a rebonding with nature, and for networks of social interaction modeled on partnership.

Goddess-centered feminist spirituality can be distinguished from other utopian or humanitarian groups on the basis of its challenge to androcentrism. As Riane Eisler puts it in *The Chalice and the Blade* (1987), "Abolitionism, pacifism, anarchism, anticolonialism, environmentalism . . . each describes different manifestations of the androcentric monster . . . the only ideology that frontally challenges [a male-dominator, female-dominated model] of human relations, as well as the principle of human ranking based on violence, is, of course, feminism."[28]

Because Goddess feminists have interpreted the advent of patriarchy as a defeat of a women-centered world, they have drawn attention to ancient history and have argued that patriarchy, from its beginnings in human history, is a cultural construction rather than a God-given reality. Because of their questions and assertions, one may imagine alternatives. Empowered by a myth of prehistoric societies modeled on partnership rather than on domination, Goddess feminism embodies a hope for something beyond the present moment. The strands of neopaganism I have been discussing thus function as a utopian poetics, a way to imagine a truly different future. Utopian poetics, in other words, point to the future and draw us toward it, suggesting alternatives that are really (not just conceptually) possible, and genuinely better than those offered by the present reality.

Goddess spirituality does not differ from other feminist spirituality in terms of its aims. All feminists hope to defeat patriarchy, and all have some way of empowering their vision. Goddess feminists base their vision on prehistoric myths and are empowered by those myths to work for a new world. The myth of an ancient matriarchy or a woman-centered religion functions for them as the historical claims about Jesus function for Christians. Goddess spirituality, like other feminist spirituality, is also deeply involved in world political matters. At the present time, a disparate group of scholars, political activists, futurists, scientists, and others have joined in a chorus of crisis, warning about the end of the world and urging humanity to choose peace and cooperation rather than war and strategic defense initiatives. Whether one reads modern science or political speeches, religion or law, cultural anthropology or poetry, it appears that we are at a new moment in human history. Mary Wakeman says, "Our present situation calls for new ways of thinking, feeling and acting in response to conditions that have arisen in, and as a result of, a context of values that is no longer sufficient to deal with its own consequences: the power to destroy ourselves."[29]

As a scholar of the ancient Near East, Wakeman is interested in the claims of Goddess feminists. She looks at the "end inherent in the beginning" of civilization and pleads for diversity, interdependence, and "the reevaluation of nature" in the future. Riane Eisler, examining the same evidence from a wider perspective, says flatly that we are at a point of evolutionary choice where we can follow a dominator model toward our own destruction or can choose a partnership paradigm for the future of the planet. Eisler's work shows how feminism provides a means to think differently about the present, and how Goddess feminism opens the mind to imagine a new future.

Whether we talk about pornography, women's ordination, or women on the American frontier, there seems to be a universal feminist assertion that modes of dominance, especially male dominance, are maladaptive. If we need a new myth of origins that will empower women and support the claim that, in the earliest moments of social interaction, humanity inhabited peaceful worlds where the gifts of men and women were equally valued, then I believe we must credit Goddess feminists for having retrieved an ancient image that could serve as a powerful engine for change.

Who is the Goddess and where does she get us? I am not sure who she is, or even if she can be named at this point. If we take the formula, "first the appearance, then the dance, then the story," to specify the proper relationship between theophany, ritual, and theology, then we can say that the theophany is prehistoric and not textually recoverable, that rituals are now being created and "rediscovered" by believers in a celebration of diversity, and that the theology has just begun to be written. Carol Christ often quotes Monique Wittig—"Make an effort to remember. Or, failing that, create"—to sanction the re-creation of Goddess rituals and beliefs. Perhaps the answer to "who is the Goddess?" needs to wait until neopagan theologians are able to be more specific. Perhaps her identity thrives on continual creativity and newness.

"Where does she get us?" As a scholar I think she gets us into a series of very interesting arguments about the nature of religious authority and the limits of historical research. As a sympathetic observer of religious communities, it appears to me that Goddess feminism presents a utopian moment in which to consider the future. Unlike traditional Western religions, which are grounded in a historical event, utopias need not have connections in a real past in order to provide hope for a real future. Goddess feminism, says Mary Wakeman, by "reaching behind the biblical monotheistic world view to affirm bodily and social processes [and to promote] natural and cultural diversity," creates a hope for new possibilities.[30] Goddess feminists use their rituals as moments of celebration, as a means of connection with the natural world, and as energy centers whence they emerge to seek the transformation of the world. Whoever she is, therefore, the Goddess invites us to criticize the present and to create a new future.

SPIRITUAL WORK

The Practice of Prayer in a Hectic World

This essay was prepared for the conference "Women and Work" presented by the women's studies program of Villanova University in March 1991. Since the focus of the conference was on practical matters, I was not surprised to see that public policy issues, comparable worth, single parenting, affirmative action, poverty, and working conditions (American and third world) dominated the program. I was surprised to find myself included in the conference, and as I prepared for it I began to wish that I had not accepted the invitation. I was supposed to be practical and kept thinking of my task as a spiritual equivalent of "news you can use," which had the overall effect of making me feel increasingly inadequate.

Women have taken so many different paths in their attempts to define a satisfactory spiritual life for themselves that I found it hard to imagine generic suggestions. But since sharing of our experiences is sometimes helpful, and since my own often ambiguous experience has been relieved by contemplating some of the spiritual classics of my own tradition, I decided to focus on the aspects of spirituality that tend to distress and comfort me. Whether they would serve some useful function for other women, I could not begin to guess, but the very exercise of choosing and articulating my own experiences in the light of parts of the Catholic tradition was salutary.

I began with the assumption that spiritual life is rooted in desire and activated by the events of our everyday lives. At this point in my life, the *events that overpower my sense of spiritual longing are the shadow sides of desire: I am sometimes more aware of fear, restlessness, and midlife crisis than I am of comfort, quietness, and communion. I connect these locations of spiritual unease with certain texts. The relentlessness of the "hound of heaven" is a good image of fear; Augustine's reflections on innate spiritual desire locate restlessness in the language of spiritual quest; and Dante, lost in the dark woods at the foot of Mount Purgatory, is a vivid image of midlife crisis. Other women will have other texts, which is all to the good: the more stories we can share as we try to understand our spiritual lives, the richer we will be.*

My stories are tied up with my attempts to come to deeper understandings of the kinds of questions raised in the context of my work. New Catholic Women *was informed by a tension I felt within myself and within my professional life. It appeared to me that religious studies professionals were not prepared to take feminism seriously and that feminists were all too eager to dismiss religious belief and practice not related to the Goddess as irrelevant or pernicious. It was hard not to believe that in order to be a feminist one had to reject organized religion, and it was particularly difficult to sustain the belief that one could be a feminist and a practicing Catholic without losing her identity. The essays in this book have all attempted to address this tension by assuming that there are nurturing springs within traditional Catholicism that can sustain Catholic feminists as they try to work out the ambiguities of their own spiritual identities.*

My own spiritual life is full of apparent contradictions. I am sustained by the feminist critics of Catholicism and by the spiritual classics of that tradition. I am attracted to the practical piety of those whose lives testify to their beliefs through constructive action in the world, and I am a closet contemplative who is powerfully drawn to silent prayer. I understand the medieval desire for nada *(nothing) that characterizes the* via negativa, *and I find in stories and images the best representations of the divine in my life. Thus this final essay is in many ways an act of faith.*

When I considered the practical suggestions I was supposed to make, I realized that I had nothing to say that had not been said thousands of times in hundreds of religious traditions. How do we nourish the life of the spirit within us so that we recognize our inner longings for what they are? How do we let the fruits of spiritual connection flow out into the daily vicissitudes of our lives? The traditional suggestions of the world's religions are difficult to follow because they are so simple: prayer draws us toward the object of our desire; fasting helps us to sort through competing goods; and almsgiving draws us back to interactions with the world we inhabit. The challenge is to find ways to articulate these practices in new language and appropriate them in new ways that suit our particular situations.

Throughout this book, I have suggested that women need to find new places for themselves, new expressions of religious language and celebration, new attributes of divine life. At the same time, I keep returning to old sources, traditional articulations of spiritual longing, and ancient manifestations of divine/human interaction. My way of coming to terms with my feminist critical instincts and my Catholic spiritual preferences is rooted in this constant traveling back and forth between new ideas and old wellsprings of sustenance. Some things will not change: we will periodically find ourselves in dry and lifeless places, longing for something we cannot articulate, and frustrated by the lack of support we receive from institutional authorities. We all have to negotiate those times in our own ways. I simply want to suggest that we not bypass those "springs of water" that can be found in various sectors of our traditions.

The challenge to reflect upon "a spirituality for women who work" is daunting because it involves all of us. As working women, our lives are surrounded with expectations. Everything we do is supposed to bear fruit but not cost very much. Women who work at home rearing children and attending to various household tasks are expected to provide something that is absolutely essential yet costs nothing, like the air we breathe. Women who work in factories, in retail sales, in offices, and in the professions find that they, too, are expected to provide invaluable, unrecognized, and unrewarded services as a matter of course.

Whether our labor is paid or unpaid, whether we work in the public or private sector, we are there to give our colleagues some amazing gifts: in addition to our duties, we are often asked to supply emotional attention, friendliness, availability at a moment's notice, and occasional (some might say, continual) subservience. We must do our job or pursue our profession, but we are also asked to heal wounds, to fix things, to feel responsible for everything, to give "the women's point of view" when it is called for, and sometimes to give sexual favors or opportunities for flirtation. Furthermore, we are to have no needs or demands that we are not willing to renounce for the benefit of others, and we are expected to bear up, lend a hand, and be unobtrusive. We may be managers or executives or professors, but in relation to those who supervise us, we are supposed to be there, cheerfully ready to take up the slack and to come through imaginatively in a crisis.

The work of women represents the most encompassing human capacity because it involves and mobilizes the entire person. It is also, as we know all too well, the most dismally rewarded and appreciated. Male philosophers coin phrases—"virtue is its own reward"—and female workers embody them. In some ineluctable way, sacrificial dedication is supposed to be our compensation: employers, lovers, pastors, and children assume that we either have very few needs or that we have our own esoteric ways to fill them. Although these same people may now realize that we need more money, more time for ourselves, or more support around the house, it may not occur to them (or even to us) that some of our deepest needs are spiritual.

We long to turn the remarkable qualities we bring to the workplace to our own advantage. In everyday terms, we want to find ways to overcome the psychic isolation we may encounter in the fatigue of too many expectations. We yearn for something "more" in our lives. We may think of it in terms of peacefulness or as a room of our own, an escape from a frantic life or a space to pursue our own thoughts; but often these images are not sufficient to describe what we *really* want. Furthermore, we may lack the vocabulary to express these deep and persistent needs. If they are "spiritual," we may feel mystified by them, not knowing how to meet them.

Let me suggest the image of hunger to begin our reflection on spirituality. If spirituality is a hunger, then many of us are simply famished. If that image makes sense, if we can relate to an unspoken need within us as an appetite, then we have already begun a religious self-reflection. In the best sense of the word, this is "spiritual work": it involves the entire person and requires a tolerance for ambiguity.

A Collection of Questions

Spirituality is hard to define. For some, it is faith made explicit in life, a definition that presumes a belief in something or a relationship with some form of organized religion, both of which have become vexed areas in light of feminist criticism. I find it more helpful to think of spirituality as intimacy, a need for a particular kind of tenderness. Spirituality is rooted in desire. We long for something we can neither name nor describe, but which is no less real because of our inability to capture it with words. The questions that cluster around this yearning are basic: What is it? Where is it? How do I find it? What do I do with it? Why am I sometimes afraid of it? How do I feel about it? How can I use my own experience to articulate it and respond to it?

For me, the most salient metaphor for spiritual life is the quest, and the best place to start is with our own experience. The idea that one begins a spiritual quest from her own experience is as ancient as the world, though until recently, men's experience and men's lives have been considered normative, whereas women's personal contributions have been judged unimportant or unworthy. For example, in the Middle Ages, when monks wanted to draw on maternal imagery to emphasize the importance of nurturance in the spiritual life, they did not consult actual mothers whose experiences of pregnancy, parturition, and parenting might have led to some new insights.[1] Instead, they either imagined Jesus in maternal terms—quite explicitly nursing them with his breasts—or drew on the writings of mystical nuns whose experience of actual motherhood was imaginative and idealized.[2] In male terms, spirituality was often coupled with mastery, with a heroic conquest of one's passions that made the journey into ethereal levels of spiritual interaction possible: the idea of using real women's lives as sources for spiritual reflection probably seemed ludicrous. Today, thanks to the women's movement and to women's burgeoning confidence in the trustworthiness of their own experience, we are not limited to male fantasies about female experience. Whatever we do, we can say that our own lives are the best and most meaningful starting points for our spiritual journeys.[3]

The Structures of Desire: Approach and Avoidance

If the shelves of bookstores reflect contemporary consciousness, it is safe to say that people today are looking for something that cannot be described in strictly material terms. We are not alone if we believe that there is something missing at the core of our existence. Whatever it is, this part of us seems to be essential and deeply personal. Popular books articulate a general need to "get in touch" with something "deep within us" and offer accessible methods of meditation and relaxation, but they are often rooted in practices that simply do not speak to us. We may be overwhelmed with the sheer variety available to those in search of "spiritual direction" or even long for a time in our past when, we imagine wistfully, things were simpler. We may believe that finding what we long for will bring us inner peace or insight, joy, or completion.

As we explore this need within us, we begin to understand that the uneasiness we feel, the desire for something more, is not rooted in our work or even in our personal lives. Frustrations we may feel in our jobs or with the inability of our friends and lovers to inhabit the private islands of our souls have very little to do with this hunger we experience. Spiritual longing therefore can be attractive, even soothing, because it takes some pressure away from other facets of our lives and leads us to ground our quest within ourselves rather than on the failures of our circumstances to fulfill us.

At the same time, spiritual desire is often accompanied by a deep sense of foreboding that makes the whole search very hard to understand in logical terms. On the one hand, since our spiritual longing is often expressed as a desire to be "happier," we anticipate the joys of understanding ourselves, or of finding some experience of love at the center of our consciousness. On the other hand, the very thought that we might be understood or loved can fill us with fear. This paradox is not peculiar to spiritual life: in normal interactions human beings long to be understood and yet dread losing control and autonomy. It is strange but true that we can experience desire and fear for the same object. When we encounter this profound contradiction in spiritual terms, it can leave us momentarily or even lingeringly paralyzed.

I am intrigued with these paradoxes because they disclose part of the shadow side of spiritual desire and describe a common experience in spirituality. Often, the more one desires spiritual fulfillment, the more her spiritual life is marked by hesitations, what psychologists would call approach/avoidance conflicts. Understanding these moments and learning to find them useful describes another aspect of "spiritual work." At this point in my own life, the shadows of the spiritual quest can be described as fear, restlessness, and midlife crisis, all normal enough to have classic images within spiritual literature.

Fear of the Lord: The Hound of Heaven

Perhaps the most haunting expression of spiritual fear comes over me when I read Francis Thompson's poem "The Hound of Heaven." No doubt the poet meant to celebrate the constancy of God's desire for us, but he does so by describing spirituality as capture. The narrator in the poem describes his flight from spiritual awakening, saying that he felt as if he were being chased by a majestic and relentless dog.

> I fled Him, down the nights and down the days;
> I fled Him, down the arches of the years;
> I fled Him, down the labyrinthine ways of my own mind;
> and in the midst of tears I hid from Him.[4]

Things come out right in the end: God is a "tremendous lover" who will not be rejected in this life and who desires that we seek genuine fulfillment in "His" arms.

I have retained the male God-language of the poet, but there is no reason for another reader to do so. The pronouns and attributes with which we make our puny descriptions of the deity need to reflect our own sense of what is desirable. Masculine language about divine persons has functioned historically to glorify male power over women and it has led to theological and spiritual systems that are misogynist and maladaptive. For those reasons, women who need the empowering language of a female divine figure must seek metaphors and images that respond to their own needs.

The masculine language of Thompson's poem, however, helps me to consider the ways in which we may indeed fear God's desire for a relationship with us. Two questions occur to me in this regard. First, I wonder if the fear of pursuit and overpowerment is more common in the spiritual writing of men than it is in that of women. Do men and women locate their spiritual fears in different places? The narrator of "The Hound of Heaven" is afraid of being overwhelmed or absorbed by the deity. Women with low self-esteem might be afraid to trust in a relationship with a divine being who loves them just as they are, an anxiety located in a sense of unworthiness, not in concern for autonomy. My second question is more troublesome. I suspect that the imagery of submission and powerlessness will not appeal to those members of society who have just begun to find their own strength. In other words, however terrifying Thompson's images may be in themselves, the notion that spirituality is a matter of submission to a relentless and powerful divine being may seem retrograde for many women. A more appealing model of spiritual life therefore might need to mute this particular aspect or find new images for the fear that seems to be part of spirituality.

Certain fears in relation to spirituality are very real and quite within our present experience, for example, the fear of disclosure. In a sophisticated world, it is possible that our own spiritual longings fill us with the fear of ridicule by our friends. We may feel that we need to keep an awakened desire for "something more" a secret: we browse through the spirituality section of the local bookstore surreptitiously, and approach a possible source of comfort—like a church service—clandestinely. Spirituality thus becomes a covert class issue, all right for certain people, but inappropriate for us. Our own search, which may be exciting or bewildering, cannot be admitted in polite company.

Another kind of spiritual fear has to do with what we imagine to be its absolute and overwhelming demands. It is not uncommon to believe we will have to pay for divine grace with a radically changed life. We cannot believe that the finding of our heart's desire will not require dramatic change in our lives, and we may resist desire for just that reason. We are not attracted to a system that might impel us to quit our jobs so that we can live with the homeless or take care of AIDS patients.

The fears we experience in the face of some kind of spiritual awakening are clues that help us to examine our needs to control situations we do not understand. Fear of God resides in a fear of ourselves, with what many spiritual writers call a disquieting emptiness at the center of our being.[5] Given a moment of solitude, in other words, we fill it up: we recall the past, we anticipate the future, we play music, we make plans, we keep busy for fear of what we may find (or not find) in the quiet spaces.

The theme of spiritual fear is a pervasive one within the literature, and we ought neither to discount it nor to be dismayed if some semblance of fearfulness gets into our attempts to respond to spiritual yearning. In bodily existence, we know that pain is a symptom; in spiritual life, fear is a symptom that can lead us to consider our attitudes and expectations in relation to a persistent and inviting divine presence that lies within us yet beyond our grasp.

Restlessness: Augustine's Romantic Quest

One classic expression of spiritual desire rooted in restlessness comes from the *Confessions* of Augustine. He began that great autobiographical reflection with this sentence: "Thou hast made us for Thyself and our hearts are restless until they rest in Thee." Having spent much of his life searching for wisdom, or for a set of practices that could lead him to inner peace, or for a community of intellectual friends with whom to share his deepest aspirations, Augustine finally realized that the promises of various philosophical and religious systems could not withstand the weight of his expectations. He had hoped to achieve an ideal life, to overcome the antagonism he felt between the flesh and the spirit, and he could not do it. Nor, he said, could *anyone* do it. The tension between physical and spiritual desires, he came to believe, could not be resolved in this life. Nor could one achieve perfection or constant tranquility.[6] His experience taught him that spirituality is necessarily marked by restlessness: one can neither attain nor relinquish one's deepest inner desires.

Like many of us, Augustine hoped to make spiritual progress by means of various efforts. He wanted to achieve enlightenment and found instead that the spiritual life is an endless journey. Its consolations were unpredictable and existed quite apart from human control or reproduction. Like others before and since, Augustine hoped to live in his head: he wanted to transcend feeling for the realm of pure thought, but he found that goal impossible. His spiritual life was rendered in his working out a balance in himself between his thoughts and his feelings, a formidable task for someone who was terrified of his own desires and unable to separate them from his passions. Augustine had to learn to understand *himself* and in doing so came to know that delight awakens a desire for God, that without feelings we can have no spiritual life. At the same time, because of our feelings we can never fulfill desire: spirituality is not something we achieve; it is something that we do throughout our lives with varying degrees of attention and understanding.

This image of restlessness appears in many of the great religious traditions of the world and seems particularly apropos for modern lives marked by constant change. We often have to deal with life as a series of interruptions, to find coherence where we may as we try to sustain jobs and families, or as we reenter the workplace after a long hiatus, or as we anticipate the unknown factors in a new job or a new environment. Restlessness can mark our attempts at prayer or our inabilities to get our lives organized. However we experience it, we can use it to explore our sense of internal longing, and we can be consoled by Augustine's spiritual truism: we cannot achieve perfection in this life however high-minded our intentions. We cannot find the perfect diet, rear the perfect child, move to the perfect neighborhood, or give our undivided attention to the perfect job. When we are tempted to surrender to a sense of futility, we might remember Augustine's struggles and his conviction that we are born with a thirst for transcendence and a frustrating inability to quench it, but the desire itself and its restless accompanying search characterize human life at its best and make it worthwhile.

Midlife Crisis: Dante Lost in the Woods

The image that becomes more real to me every year is one in the opening lines of "Hell," the first book of Dante's *Divine Comedy*. "Midway this way of life we're bound upon, I woke to find myself in a dark wood where the right road was wholly lost and gone." He goes on to say that the mere memory of the experience stirs fear in his blood, but that in the bitterness of the experience, he gained such insight that he will take it upon himself to write it down. *The Divine Comedy* is the story of Dante's spiritual journey through hell, purgatory, and heaven, and one need not be a middle-aged Catholic to appreciate it.[7] The *Comedy* tells us what it means to confront our inner demons, to see how our own particular responses to love and refusals of love determine our place in the cosmic design.

I find "Hell" helpful for three reasons: it locates spiritual awakening in a midlife crisis, it values the power of romantic love, and it pictures sin in realistic and understandable terms. According to his own assessment, Dante was born with great talents but turned his back on them as he chased after everything under the sun and filled his life with broken promises and empty dreams. His spiritual awakening occurred in the midst of betrayals, which he pictures as being lost in a dark woods. In other words, when he was penniless, in disgrace, middle-aged, and hopeless, he finally turned toward God. This turning of his soul was not automatic or instantaneous. On the contrary. He was able to escape from his miserable situation only by way of a mysterious tour of the underworld, what today we would call a frightening excursion into the byways of the soul (or psyche). And he was empowered to make that journey because once, as a young man, he had the ordinary yet extraordinary experience of falling in love.[8]

When we fall in love with another person, we are touched by God in a way that can never be obliterated: we know ourselves best in that moment. If we respond to that love, then we will find that what we want for ourselves and what God wants for us are the same thing. We need not fear human love or forsake human poetry since both are moments of grace, mediations of the divine that we can partake of and understand. If we spurn love or ignore it, we will find ourselves mired in our own egos, lost. Escape requires merciless self-examination and a cold, hard look at the reality of personal sin.

Spirituality is not simply a story of success. If it were, then we would not agonize about it as we do. Dante suggests that spirituality springs from mutual desire and is meant to be a relationship between lover and beloved, where God and the soul play interchangeable parts. Sin is the refusal of mutuality, the spurning of love in real human terms and thus in cosmic ones as well. This refusal can be rooted in rebellion, fear, ego, stubbornness, anger, ignorance, laziness, or the distractions of an overstuffed life. Dante's "Hell" is a series of images designed to explain these sins and to warn us against them even as it shows how easy it is to slip into them.

Cosmic Connections

As I have described spirituality grounded in desire and explored some of its concomitant shadows, I have articulated it as a longing for a relationship with God. It could very well be, however, that women feel cornered by the patriarchal baggage that surrounds that word and that concept and feel constrained to find a new way for themselves. I am not sure we need to worry about the location of the sources of our religious nurturance. We do, however, have to find some way to respond to the yearning, to get in touch with the quiet center of ourselves. Religion is what we do with our solitude, says Whitehead. I sustain that solitude with the classics of Western Christianity; others follow the practices of Buddhism, the harmonies of Navaho religion, or some combination of religious insights that suits their individual needs.

However we name the object of our yearning or choose the practices that help us get in touch with it, we should recognize that we are already joined to what we desire. God—Source of All Being, Eternal Word, Creative Spirit, Fountain of Holiness, Mystical Rose—is at the heart of the creative process that touches our everyday lives, and we are at the heart of the creative process that touches the life of God.[9] What we do—in our work, in our lives, in our conversations, in our choices for ourselves—touches God in a profound way. Creator and creation are joined in the countless interactive events that make up the life of the universe.

We do not live and work in isolation: what we do contributes to or detracts from the creation of new life in the universe. The chaos and order we experience in our own lives is part of the process and a reflection of it. Our work, therefore, is part of the partnership that contributes to the continuation of the world. The spirit of God moves through history and is not absent from its development. The constant energy of the universe, from subatomic particle movement to galactic explosions, includes us. What we hope to achieve in our own personal lives and in the human community also defines what we should hope for in relation to the universe: "the art of intimacy and distance, the capacity of beings to be totally present to each other while further affirming and enhancing the differences and identities of each."[10]

In many ways, this cosmic goal is similar to our spiritual hope. We want to be related to that which stirs our deepest desires. We want intimacy and we need distance; we long to be totally present but experience that longing fleetingly in the middle of a busy and distracted life; we want to be affirmed and respected for our differences and yet participate in the life of that divine being who somehow holds the key to our own self-discovery.

Some Practical Considerations

Assuming that we feel an inner longing—whether we can articulate it or not, whether we prefer one way to describe it over another— what can we actually *do* about it? How do we respond to it? How do we get ourselves in shape to recognize it? How do we let the results of our spiritual life overflow into the world around us? The traditional answers in almost all religions are simple enough and yet, paradoxically, difficult: *prayer* orients us toward the center of our being; *fasting* helps us to pay attention to competing desires; and *almsgiving* keeps us in touch with the broken world we inhabit.

When I think about these spiritual disciplines in practical terms, I am often reminded of losing weight. The remedy for obesity sounds simple—eat less and get more exercise—but it is not easy because our minds and wills do not govern all aspects of our lives. However fully we are in control of our exterior lives, we are often tangled in our feelings and in the turmoil of our subconscious lives. Good spiritual health, like good physical health, requires that we examine the dark corners of our lives and befriend those parts of ourselves that disturb us. The continuing work of integration that we do—in our friendships or in our communities, with lovers or in therapy settings—is a necessary concomitant to the ancient practices of spiritual systems.

The practices themselves are generic answers that have vast literatures to explain how they work, why they are important, what God expects in relation to them, what pitfalls one might encounter in attempting them, and so forth. Most of the religions of the world have developed various techniques to enhance spiritual practice, and most of them offer a variety of interpretations along with ancient and ongoing arguments about the ways to pray, to give alms, and to fast. Since the specifics of practice appeal to people in highly personal ways, I will discuss these ancient spiritual disciplines only in very general terms.

Almsgiving is an ancient recognition that we have some responsibilities to people who have less than we do. It is a community concept that we try to live out in an individualistic world. Almost all religions require their believers to share some portion of their goods with those less fortunate than themselves. The amount given away need not be large, as the gospel story of the "widow's mite" tells us, but the intention ought to be motivated by generosity not by grandiosity. The most familiar measure of religious giving is the tithe, usually taken as a 10 percent share of the money we earn. Some people compute their percentage on the basis of their gross salary and some on their "take home pay."

On the whole, Roman Catholics have not taken to tithing as religiously as many Protestants. An older Catholic once told me that tithing was "against his religion," the same argument he advanced to excuse himself from congregational singing. For some Catholic women, the idea of giving their money to an institution that continues discriminatory practices against them is counterproductive. Tithing, however, does not specify the object of our giving, it simply says that we must part with some of our income for the good of others. Those who do not want to give money to a church have other options in today's world.[11]

I believe that we should consider tithing our time as well as our money. If we give 10 percent of our money to some kind of charitable institution, we could also give 10 percent of our work hours (about four each week) to someone who needs it. These demands are minimal, but that does not make them easy. Money needs to be given away responsibly and quickly so we do not trip over our own bountiful spirits. Volunteer time is harder to figure out and may need to be given to ourselves or our children or parents rather than to agencies within the community. The practice is not as important as the attitude: almsgiving is a means of cosmic connection, it should tell us where we are in the universal scheme of things, and it should raise our consciousness about the needs of others. If tithing causes resentment rather than stirring compassion, there is probably something wrong with what we are doing, a clue that calls us to reexamine our practice.

Fasting is a healthful practice in some religions and a spiritual discipline in others. It makes sense to me only as a way to focus attention on the distractions of life and to sharpen our appetites so that we have a better understanding of who we are. Traditionally those on a spiritual quest refrain from indulging themselves: they fast from food or water or sex or sleep. When we do not eat all day, we learn what it means to be hungry and can have, perhaps, a brief first-hand experience of what the majority of the world's peoples know as a matter of course. Again, the attitude is as important as the practice: fasting is an ascetic action, a way to train oneself to see more than is ordinarily available.

Fasting is a spiritual discipline that seems to many people to be irrelevant in the modern world. Some see it as enhancing diet consciousness, but as a religious practice it often arouses suspicion, as if people who do it might also find other ways to "mortify" their flesh. The very notion of mortification is malodorous to many Catholic women because the old stories of female saints are encrusted with examples of nauseating penances recommended to women by their male confessors. Fasting, however, is not meant to humiliate us; and if that is its general effect, then we need to find other means of drawing ourselves away from the distractions of our everyday lives so that we have the time and space to look at ourselves in relation to God.

John of the Cross says that the fast is sauce for the feast. Fasting is supposed to enhance our appetites, sharpen our senses so that we can accept the simple gifts of food, drink, and fellowship with humility and gratitude rather than with a sense of entitlement. In a consumer culture, fasting might be a way to make an occasional choice away from the mall and toward something else (a visit to a shut-in, a walk in the park). It might mean a thoughtful refusal to buy everything we can afford. Whatever we choose to do or not do in this area, our practice should be evaluated periodically in light of our spiritual desires.

If almsgiving helps us to understand where we are and fasting tunes our perceptions of who we are, *prayer* is our response to desire: it helps us to be who we are in the presence of God. When people talk about spiritual yearning, they often think about getting into themselves, getting in touch with the centers of their existence. Teresa of Avila says that the object of our desire exists *within* us waiting to be discovered. Prayer helps us to find that treasure, but there is no formula for prayer that works for everyone. The religions of the world offer a vast array of possibilities, which can be classified as three general types of prayer: mantras, postures, and mental activities.

A mantra is a repetitious sentence or word that is supposed to fill the mind and heart with the divine presence. Franny Glass, in J. D. Salinger's novel *Franny and Zooey*, dropped out of school and locked herself away in her room to practice the mantric advice she read in a classic spiritual text, *The Way of the Pilgrim.*[12] In that book, a Russian pilgrim who decides to follow the biblical injunction to "pray without ceasing" learns to recite the Jesus prayer—"Lord Jesus Christ, have mercy on me"—12,000 times a day, in conjunction with his breathing and his heartbeat. That mantric practice changed his entire life, which is what attracted Salinger's heroine, and what attracts students of the text today. Muslims recite the thousand beautiful names for God in the same way. The repetition is not mindless: on the contrary, it is supposed to occupy one's total physical and spiritual attention until it becomes second nature, until the words and the divine presence are joined within the person using the prayer.

Religious postures, a second general type of prayer, require physical acts of some kind: for example, breathing, yogic postures, standing or sitting in a certain way, or making a pilgrimage to a holy place. Again, the concentration is on the union of thought and action: one tries to express physically what one longs for spiritually. Physical activities are meant, often, to draw the participant into a trance in which she can hear God's voice or come to a deeper understanding of the divine will. Many people are aware of Yoga as a form of exercise but not as a form of spiritual connection, yet it is an ancient prayer form that combines breathing and posture so that one can be more closely in touch with the spiritual forces that shape one's life.

Mental prayer is probably the form most familiar to us. Here one is essentially quiet and hopes to draw close to the object of her desire. One can pray quietly by way of meditation or contemplation, the difference being in the use or nonuse of images. In meditation one pictures certain religious figures or actions—one might picture

Mary at the foot of the cross, for example, or Jesus at the Last Sup-per—and let herself be drawn into the representation. In contem-plation one tries to drop into a total silence where no pictures, im-ages, sounds, or anything else distracts from the communion between the soul and God. Mental prayer is supposed to enable us to get into the centers of our beings. Some imagine that task taking a lifetime, and others believe it is possible to do it in a matter of minutes—differences that probably reflect disparate religious auto-biographies and personal dispositions.

Prayer is a deeply personal response to the desires of the heart in relation to the divine being. It is also a spiritual discipline that re-quires time and attention and is fraught with difficulty. Some people have developed the habit of prayer over many years and seem to drop into it easily and often, but they, too, experience times of darkness and aridity, noise and distraction that inhibit them. No one reciting a mantra, practicing a spiritual posture, or sitting in meditation is *always* present to that activity, and one learns to avoid particular pitfalls only to encounter new ones. But the very act of praying—in whatever form, with or without words—is the key to prayer. Some people begin their prayer by reading Scripture or reflecting on the Psalms; some keep a journal; others just sit quietly expecting noth-ing in particular. There is no right way to do it, and those who have tried and failed might remember that great saints like Teresa of Avila had trouble praying, too. In a book written for the sisters in her community she says, "There is no other remedy for this evil of giving up prayer than to begin again," talking not about them so much as about herself. [13]

Conclusion

The general burgeoning of interest in spirituality in the past few years coupled with a dissatisfaction with traditional forms of West-ern religion has led many people on fascinating spiritual journeys. If practice is a measure of religiosity, women have always been more religious than men, and it is no surprise that women's ideas and questions are in the forefront of new movements of spirituality. I find the attempts to reimagine the divine being in feminist terms both healthy and attractive precisely because they draw women back to a spiritual life even when they are alienated from their religious heritage. It is too soon to tell whether the questions and practices, feelings and frustrations of the new spiritualities are any different from the old ones. I am assuming that they are similar, and that the restlessness expressed by Augustine's famous prayer is as relevant now as it was in the fourth century. I believe that the longing for something more is universal and that people who yearn to pursue their heart's desire are as fearful and sinful now as they were in the Middle Ages.

Spiritual work is an internal labor of love that taps into our deepest desires. It brings us face to face with ourselves and, in some measure, with the divine reality of the universe, whatever name we give it or however we pursue it. Spirituality for women who work is no different from spirituality for those who have given their lives in pursuit of spiritual illumination; it helps us to take a long, loving look at the Real in ways that can transform our lives and satisfy a buried hunger.

EPILOGUE

The Nuns' Chapel

Many years ago I visited a large Catholic seminary that had many
different chapels. The spiritual director was delighted with the postconciliar chapel with its movable furniture: he explained that by
changing the configuration of the furniture, he could embody the
church as "ever changing, ever new." The rector, on the other hand,
was most at home in the main church, built in the early part of the
twentieth century and distinguished by an enormous fresco surrounding the high altar featuring Christ in the vestments of a Roman
Catholic priest. The students were drawn to a variety of mini-chapels
where they could meditate in silence and experiment with different
prayer forms. As I was walking around the outside with a friend, I
looked up and saw what appeared to be small stained-glass windows
tucked away in the back of the main building. When I asked what
was up there, he said, "Oh, that was the nuns' chapel." I was fascinated, and he took me to see this small, out-of-the-way place built
long ago to serve the spiritual needs of the women who cooked and
cleaned for the priests and seminarians. Since the women themselves
were long gone, the space was no longer used.

I came back to that chapel several times over the next few days,
not sure what attracted me to it. Although I experienced a great
peacefulness at first, I began to feel increasingly smothered by its

design. The nuns' chapel was a celebration of and exhortation to male models of femininity. It was hidden and modest. The small windows offered no vision of the outside world: they opened only a little bit and only onto an air corridor. More important, the windows offered colorful praise to one or another of the so-called feminine virtues: they honored "humility" and "meekness" and quietly reminded sisters of their obligations to "generosity" and "service." All the furniture was diminutive, so much so that to this day I recall it in miniature. The altar itself was very small, as were the pews and credence table and tabernacle. The altar vessels were simple and serviceable rather than flashy and grand (as they were in the main church). The tiny confessionals might have been placed there to embody Vincent McNabb's old joke about hearing nuns' confessions. "It is like being nibbled to death by ducks," he is supposed to have said.[1]

I have thought about that chapel many times in the past twenty years, especially as I consider spiritual resources for Catholic women. My first reaction to it was positive: I was powerfully drawn to the peacefulness of the place, the fact that it was set aside for women. I can imagine that those women in the Catholic church who still find their spiritual nourishment in the devotional life that was popular before the Second Vatican Council would be comfortable there. Within a short time, however, I felt uneasy in that space, finding it too small, too restrictive, and slightly ominous. My conversations with Catholic feminists lead me to believe that they would share this general feeling of wariness, perhaps might even feel a strong urge to get away from that place as soon as possible and never return to it.

In light of the disturbing questions one confronts with a raised consciousness, it is hard to imagine returning to that nuns' chapel. I shudder when I remember it. The furniture seems to have been designed to make me believe that I am small, or if I am not, that I ought to be. The absence of fresh air and any way to gaze out into the world appears planned to keep me contained and my ambitions under control. The windows—with their constant exhortations to service and humility—seem placed there to remind me of my subservience. I would not attempt anything at the altar in that chapel except to freshen its flowers. My sense of vocation in that place would probably be of one who must be content to accept secondary status, finding it a privilege to cook for and otherwise care for fathers (husbands or priests).

Both as a metaphor and in reality, the nuns' chapel is a place many Catholic women need to get away from. In that feeling, they are not alone. In 1832 Elizabeth Cady Stanton led an exodus of women from her Presbyterian church as an eager young minister waxed eloquent on 1 Timothy 2:12.[2] One hundred and thirty-nine years later, Mary Daly, preaching to a full chapel at Harvard Divinity School, convinced a significant number of her hearers that the Moses story was paradigmatic: they followed her out of the building and out of the church.[3]

The community of women who exist outside of these chapels—whether their confinement is metaphorical or real—are no less desirous of a relationship with God. The ideas that inform this book are predicated on the belief that women on the margins of their tradition are pioneers in a new kind of spiritual awareness. They may be in the process of creating new places for themselves, or they may simply be wandering and wondering. They may be settling in or on a journey. In my essay for the Women's Ordination Conference, I imagined women "called to a new land," and in my essay for the Villanova Theology Institute I tried to make sense of existence in the desert. In my later essays, I have tried to imagine what it would mean to find sustenance in the wellsprings of the Catholic tradition. All of these tasks are parts of spiritual existence.

In many religions, as I've said, spirituality is described in terms of a quest, a journey through an underworld or toward a heavenly destination. Stories of religious heroes talk of pilgrimage, a term that can describe a physical journey to a holy place or a spiritual adventure within the labyrinths of one's own soul. In the Jewish and Christian traditions, the concept of spiritual journey has sometimes been described in relation to the wilderness. Wandering through or being lost in a desert has been a powerful, biblically based metaphor for important moments in one's spiritual life.

The ancient Hebrews dramatically liberated by Yahweh from the slavery of Egypt had to wander forty years in the deserts of the Sinai peninsula before entering the promised land. The story of their wanderings, understood as an extension of the *exodus*, has been particularly moving for marginalized people seeking to escape bondage. The defeat of the Jews by the Babylonians and the ensuing *exile* is a later and perhaps even more powerful way of understanding a yearning for new life in a barren environment. Exile stories have been powerful metaphors for spirituality because they tell of a temporary displacement and promise renewal. In the desert of the exile one yearns most of all to return home.

When I think about spirituality for Catholic feminists, I am often drawn to desert parallels. For a long time I thought there were major psychological differences between exodus and exile: one was associated with liberation from captivity whereas the other was related to purification and new life. One saw spiritual life in terms of escape from bondage while the other imagined it as "coming home" after a long sojourn in a hazardous place. In feminist terms, I tended to think about "reformers" of the tradition as those "in exile," whereas the "revolutionaries," like the Hebrews escaping from Pharaoh, were described best in terms of an "exodus" experience. Revisionary feminists were in exile from patriarchy, gathered in the desert, searching for a fuller articulation of spiritual life or community celebration, yearning to come home. Radical feminists had rejected any hope for revision and had left biblical and ecclesiastical authority behind as they searched in the desert for a new religious dimension or for a rediscovery of a religion predating patriarchy.

As I considered it further, however, it occurred to me that it does not really matter whether one sees herself in a desert learning new songs and yearning to return "home" or whether one sees herself in a desert wandering toward some new woman-affirming religion. Exile or exodus, it is still a desert we are in as we search for ways to understand the deepest centers of our lives. Whether we eventually "go home" or finally move to a radically new place is not altogether important. What are we going to do *now?* Where do we look for clues? What does it mean to use women's experience as a norm against which to measure religious language, textual traditions, and the needs for communion? How do we forge a new spirituality in the context of our own particular time and place?

Spirituality is faith made explicit in life, an expression of one's deepest convictions with respect to the ultimate. It is therefore best expressed in the relationships one has with others, with the created order, and with the divine. Wherever we find ourselves on a continuum of belief and celebration, we need to trust our intuitions, share our insights, and learn as much as we can from one another as we try to find our way out of the wilderness. The Hebrews during the exodus complained about the hardships they faced and wondered if they were wise in leaving Egypt behind. The Jews during the exile sat weeping as they remembered their lost homeland. In both instances, Yahweh's re-creative power and their own brave responses to divine initiative led to new moments in their religious development. In both instances, they learned to redefine their situation.

Catholic feminist spirituality may mean redefining the wilderness to include the experiences of women inside and outside the institutional church. Since the religious autobiographies of Catholic women are diverse, we cannot really talk about *a* spirituality for Catholic women. At best we can learn to listen to Catholic women with a wide variety of experiences and expectations, to find in their lives some resources for ourselves as we begin to identify our own spiritual needs more clearly. Those in a wilderness usually realize that their first challenge is survival, a requirement that has been felt and addressed in different ways by Catholic feminists.

The roads along which many Catholic women try to survive or to find new life are marked on the left by those who have rejected the tradition altogether in an effort to find a more satisfying community of religious celebration. They are marked on the right by those who are content within the tradition as it is or who yearn for a return to the church as it was before the intrusions of postconciliar pluralism. Catholic feminists, for the most part, are not defined by the extremes of the spectrum. Neither totally rejecting nor totally accepting of the Catholic church and its tradition, they attempt to find a modus vivendi by which they can somehow blend the best insights of Catholicism with the new perspectives offered to them by feminism. Some are drawn to a radically incarnational spirituality modeled on liberationist themes, whereas others seek spiritual solace within the contemplative poetry of a struggle with the absolute. Still others attempt to forge some sort of eclectic or revisionary spirituality that marks them as Catholics even as it affirms them as feminists.

In metaphorical and real ways, Catholic feminists are building the future, perhaps by building new chapels on the grounds of the church we can neither abandon nor attend comfortably. If we want to reclaim our tradition and generate renewal, then it is probably wise not to lose touch with the institutional church. At the same time, we clearly need alternative spaces in which to regenerate ourselves. Someday these chapels might be actual places, but today they exist mostly as states of mind, shelters for those who value diversity and pluralism, sanctuaries for those who perceive a truly catholic future.

In these new chapels, we might gather with those who are either uncomfortable or unwelcome in the main church. We worship a deity whose interactions and attributes are much richer than what has been preserved for us in patriarchal traditions, whose names are multiple, whose gender metaphors are both masculine and feminine. We honor female saints and have images of Mary that go beyond the mother and child motifs that now dominate her story. We may not have fixed pews and imposing pulpits, and the spatial design will make it possible both to see one another and to create focal points as the need arises.

Since the Creator is present in the material realities of our lives, we will be a sacramental people who no longer accept a vision of reality that separates the sacred from the profane. We do not "go to church" in order to fortify ourselves for jobs "in the world," rather church *is* our presence in the world. Because a church ministers to those who suffer, we attempt to provide a safe space for those imperiled by the forces of evil in the world. Since we know from experience that oppression stems from conditions in which one group has power over another, a good feminist consciousness can only strengthen this vocation of service.

In this new chapel, we celebrate with old ceremonies and we write new ones to include the visions of others. We sing in many voices and pray in many postures. Nourished by ancient stories and by new ones, we raise a fuss. Remembering the stories that began this book, we raise a fuss in the name of Mary O'Donnell and Elizabeth Miller and all women in the past who were cramped by male ideas of "womanhood" and told to be silent. We raise a fuss in the name of Annette Anderson and Patricia Reily and all women in the present who are trying to find a space without anguish in which to celebrate themselves spiritually and politically while remaining vital members of the Catholic tradition. Finally, we raise a fuss by standing firm against those who would return us to the deadly embrace of the past in the name of all the women of the future who will look back on our day to see what stories we remembered, what resources kept us going.

Preface

1. "Letter to the Bishops on the Pastoral Care of Homosexual Persons" was issued by the Congregation for the Doctrine of the Faith on 31 October 1986. For a reprint of the letter plus reactions to it from scholars, pastors, and others, see Jeannine Gramick and Pat Furey, eds., *The Vatican and Homosexuality* (New York: Crossroad Publishing, 1988).

2. See, for example, A. Kosnik et al., *Human Sexuality: New Directions in American Catholic Thought* (New York: Paulist Press, 1977).

Chapter 1. At Home in Her Own House

1. Teresa of Avila, *The Book of Her Life* 40.5, in *The Collected Works of Teresa of Avila*, trans. Kieran Kavanaugh, O.C.D., and Otilio Rodriguez, O.C.D. (Washington, D.C.: Institute of Carmelite Studies, 1976), 1:278.

2. Constance Fitzgerald, "A Discipleship of Equals: Voices from Tradition—Teresa of Avila and John of the Cross," in *A Discipleship of Equals: Towards a Christian Feminist Spirituality*, ed. Francis A. Eigo (Villanova, Pa.: Villanova University Press, 1988), p. 83.

3. By equality here I mean that Teresa experienced her relationship with God as a partnership in which both God and the soul need one another and provide loving space for one another. Spiritual equality with God, classically expressed in autotheistic language, has been a matter of dispute in Christian history. Late medieval mystics like Meister Eckhart and Jan van Ruusbroec sometimes expressed their union with God as an identity with God and were criticized severely for such language. Catherine of Genoa, in the sixteenth century, said simply, "My *me* is God." What this language meant to these mystics and whether it should be condemned or affirmed by the Catholic tradition is the subject of a recent article. See James A. Wiseman, "To Be God with God: The Autotheistic Sayings of the Mystics," *Theological Studies* 51 (1990): 230–51.

4. Fitzgerald, "A Discipleship of Equals," p. 73.

5. See Constance Fitzgerald, "Impasse and the Dark Night," in *Women's Spirituality: Resources for Christian Development*, ed. Joann Wolski Conn (New York: Paulist Press, 1986), pp. 287–312.

6. Betty Friedan, *The Feminine Mystique* (New York: Dell Publishing, 1963). By noting the impact of Friedan's work, I do not mean to imply that there was no women's movement before the sixties. The first sounds of feminist criticism in America were sounded in 1846 at the first Women's Rights Convention in Seneca Falls, New York. The importance and power of the work of those pioneers carried the women's movement through the early years of the twentieth century to the passage of the nineteenth amendment, securing the vote for women. Dale Spender argues that there has *always* been a women's movement, just sometimes a little muted. Others say that the movement all but evaporated after women got the vote so that the reemergence of women's issues in the late fifties was a new initiative.

7. Ruth Rosen, "The Need for Memory," *Tikkun* 2 (1987): 51. Rosen's article is an excellent appraisal of the territory of sixties feminism, and I am indebted to her for my encapsulation of the fifties and her insight that sixties feminists were refugees from the *zeitgeist* of the fifties.

8. Ibid.

9. Ibid., p. 52.

10. Ibid.

11. One of the clear connections between modern feminism and political action can be found in the alliances with the ecological movement. Theologians, activists, practitioners of neopaganism, and more traditional communitarians all see feminism and "women's ways of living" intimately bound to the survival of life on earth.

12. *One in Christ Jesus: A Pastoral Response to the Concerns of Women for Church and Society*, as found in *Origins* 19 (5 April 1990), para. 132. There has now been a third draft of the pastoral letter (May 1991), but the process and outcome of the letter are highly contested. Eugene Kennedy, in the *National Catholic Reporter* 28 (20 September 1991): 6, suggested that the bishops scrap the letter on women and, instead, write one on *men*. My purpose here is not to do an analysis of the letter in its different versions, but to suggest that the relationship between the Roman Catholic hierarchy and Catholic feminists continues to be a vexed one.

13. Rosemary Ruether, "Dear U.S. Bishops, you insult our intelligence," in *National Catholic Reporter* 27 (18 May 1990): 16.

14. Mary Jo Weaver, *New Catholic Women: A Contemporary Challenge to Traditional Religious Authority* (San Francisco: Harper and Row, 1985).

15. Carol P. Christ, "Symbols of Goddess and God in Feminist Theology," in *The Book of the Goddess*, ed. Carl Olson (New York: Crossroad Publishing, 1983), p. 231.

16. Sallie McFague, *Models of God: Theology for an Ecological, Nuclear Age* (Philadelphia: Fortress Press, 1987), p. ix. McFague's work has been devoted to an examination of the ways in which metaphors and models function in religious language. Her reconceptualization of the Trinity replaces Father, Son, and Holy Spirit with God the Mother, God the Lover, and God the Friend.

17. See Peter Brown, *Augustine of Hippo* (London: Faber and Faber, 1967).

18. I have explored some of the problems connected with Goddess religion in chapter 5. The problems of historicity are major stumbling blocks to those who prefer their religious belief to be grounded on clear historical data of some kind. For an extensive look at some of these problems, see Rosemary Ruether, *Gaia and God: An Ecofeminist Theology of Earth-Healing* (San Francisco: Harper and Row, 1992), especially chapter 6. Ruether questions the historical sources for Goddess religion and also criticizes the Goddess symbols themselves, which, she argues, have more affinity with post-Christian Western romanticism than with anything neolithic. Jo Ann Hackett also asks if ancient Goddess figures are really appropriate symbols for religious women. See "Can a Sexist Model Liberate Us? Ancient Near Eastern 'Fertility' Goddesses," *Journal of Feminist Studies in Religion* 5 (1989): 65–76.

19. See, for example, Mary Daly, *Gyn/Ecology* (Boston: Beacon Press, 1978), pp. 57–64, passim.

20. J. D. Salinger, "Teddy," in *Nine Stories* (New York: Ballantine Books, 1953), p. 188.

21. Evelyn Underhill, *The School of Charity* (London: Longmans, Green, and Co., 1939), p. 108.

Chapter 2. In Search of the Grail

1. Alden Brown, *The Grail Movement and American Catholicism, 1940–1975* (Notre Dame, Ind.: University of Notre Dame Press, 1989).

2. See Laurence Moore, *Religious Outsiders and the Making of America* (New York: Oxford University Press, 1986).

3. Brown, *The Grail Movement*, p. 175.

4. Ibid., p. 171.

5. Linda Clark, Marian Ronan, and Eleanor Walker, *Image-Breaking Image-Building* (New York: Pilgrim Press, 1981); Susan Cady, Marian Ronan, and Hal Taussig, *Wisdom's Feast: Sophia in Study and Celebration* (San Francisco: Harper and Row, 1989).

6. Brown, *The Grail Movement*, p. 107.

7. See Riane Eisler, *The Chalice and the Blade* (San Francisco: Harper and Row, 1987).

8. Brown, *The Grail Movement*, p. 159.

9. For a portrait of the Grail by a lifetime member, see Janet Kalven, "Women Breaking Boundaries: The Grail and Feminism," *Journal of Feminist Studies in Religion* 5 (1989): 119–42.

10. Quotations from recent Grail statements come from unpublished documents, working papers prepared for specific meetings. Most of the material I have quoted from here is stored in the Grail archives in Grailville, 932 O'Bannonville Road, Loveland, Ohio. When Alden Brown wrote his book, these archives were in a very early process of organization. When I wrote this essay, I had access to the archives, but they were still not ready for scholars to use. It is not possible, therefore, to give more exact citations for the contemporary Grail material.

11. See Brown, *The Grail Movement*, p. 175.

Chapter 3. Called to a New Land

1. Genesis 12ff.

2. Most of the sources I used to write this essay are used in *New Catholic Women*, chapter 4, which covers women's ordination. Those interested in the history, technicalities, and footnotes for some of the arguments presented here may want to consult that chapter.

3. Marjorie Tuite, O.P. (1922–86), was a tireless activist on behalf of women. As director of Ecumenical Action for Church Women United and national coordinator of the National Assembly of Religious Women, she brought the painful realities of the lives of women, poor people, blacks, and Nicaraguan refugees to the attention of American women, especially to women in the American Catholic church. One of her greatest gifts was her ability to work with and understand people and their problems, and to help them to organize and assert themselves.

4. Elisabeth Schüssler Fiorenza, *In Memory of Her: A Feminist Theological Reconstruction of Christian Origins* (New York: Crossroad Publishing, 1983).

5. Still one of the best introductions to the life of Pius is E. E. Y. Hales's *Pio Nono* (New York: Doubleday, 1962).

6. Schüssler Fiorenza (see note 4) understands Jesus as a countercultural reformer. See her "Feminist Theology as a Critical Theology of Liberation," *Theological Studies* 36 (1975): 605–26.

7. See Elisabeth Schüssler Fiorenza, "Discipleship and Patriarchy: Early Christian Ethos and Christian Ethics in a Feminist Theological Perspective," in *The Annual of the Society of Christian Ethics: Selected Papers, 1982*, ed. L. Rasmussen (Waterloo, Ont.: CSR Publications, 1982), pp. 131–72.

8. Mary Bader Papa, *Christian Feminism: Completing the Subtotal Woman* (Chicago: Fides/Claretian Press, 1981), p. 186.

9. Mary Daly quotes extensively from Woolf in the last pages of *Beyond God the Father* (Boston: Beacon Press, 1973), pp. 193–98.

10. See Ralph Kiefer's review of *Ministry* by Edward Schillebeeckx, *Commonweal* 108 (1981): 327–33.

11. Rosemary Ruether, "Women's Ordination: What Is the Problem?" in *Women and the Catholic Priesthood*, ed. Anne Marie Gardiner (New York: Paulist Press, 1976), p. 33.

12. Joan Huber, "Ambiguities in Identity Transformation: From Sugar and Spice to Professor," *Notre Dame Journal of Education* 2 (1972): 338.

Chapter 4. *Springs of Water in a Dry Land*

1. Very few studies about women in the church have bothered to ask women's own opinions. As the British Laity Commission commented in its report to its bishops, "Despite the fact that very little research has been undertaken to establish how Catholic women in this country regard themselves . . . there is no shortage of authoritative statements suggesting what women should or should not be doing." See *Why Can't a Woman Be More Like a Man?* (London: Catholic Information Services, n.d.). When the American bishops decided to write a pastoral letter about women in the church, they scheduled broad-based "listening sessions," but it has been the opinion of many of the women who "testified" that their opinions were not really heard, or if heard, were minimalized. Perhaps the most helpful source for the voice of women in one segment of the American Catholic church can be found in the *Task Force Report on the Role of Women in the Church of Southeast Wisconsin*. See *Catholic Herald* (Milwaukee), Supplement, 9 December 1982.

2. See Mary O'Connell, "Pastors: Parishes Still Follow the Leader," *U.S. Catholic* 47 (1982): 17–24.

3. See Rosemary Ruether, *Women-Church: Theology and Practice* (San Francisco: Harper and Row, 1987), p. 5.

4. Walsh's book was first published in New York by the Catholic Summer School Press in 1907. It kept Catholics mindful of the age of Aquinas, papalism, and other claims to past glory. It has been reprinted continually since then and was a staple of Catholic identification with the medieval tradition throughout the first half of the twentieth century.

5. I am indebted to many general works in this area, mostly to Norman Pittinger, *Process Thought and Christian Faith* (New York: Pilgrim Press, 1979), and to Daniel Day Williams, *The Spirit and the Forms of Love* (New York: Harper and Row, 1968). For those who wish to read Whitehead directly, try *Process and Reality: An Essay in Cosmology* (New York: Social Sciences Book Store, 1941). An excellent commentary on that work is Donald W. Sherburne, ed., *A Key to Whitehead's Process and Reality* (Chicago: University of Chicago Press, 1966). A good introduction to the concepts and vocabulary used in process thought is Marjorie Hewitt Suchocki, *God, Christ, Church: A Practical Guide to Process Theology* (New York: Crossroad Publishing, 1986).

6. Williams, *Spirit and Forms of Love*, p. 106.

7. Margaret Farley, *Personal Commitments* (San Francisco: Harper and Row, 1986), p. 116.

8. Suchocki, *God, Christ, Church*, pp. 214–15.

9. Rabindranath Tagore, from *Gitanjali*. See *A Tagore Reader*, ed. Amiya Chakravarty (Boston: Beacon Press, 1966), p. 305.

Chapter 5. Who Is the Goddess and Where Does She Get Us?

1. See Elizabeth Cady Stanton, *The Woman's Bible* (1898; Seattle: Coalition Task Force on Women and Religion, 1974); Matilda Joslyn Gage, *Woman, Church and State* (1893; Watertown, Mass.: Persephone Press, 1980). Both Stanton and Gage attempt to break the link between male authority and God's will, whether that divine mandate is located in a written word (the Bible) or in an institution (the church).

2. Published in the mid-1970s, *The Feminist Book of Light and Shadow* was incorporated into Z. Budapest's two-volume *The Holy Book of Women's Mysteries* (Los Angeles: The Susan B. Anthony Coven No. 1, 1979, 1980).

3. Margot Adler, *Drawing Down the Moon: Witches, Druids, Goddess-worshippers, and Other Pagans in America Today*, revised and expanded edition (Boston: Beacon Press, 1986), and Starhawk, *The Spiral Dance: A Rebirth of the Ancient Religion of the Great Goddess*, tenth anniversary edition, with new introduction and commentary (San Francisco: Harper and Row, 1989).

4. Rosemary Ruether, *New Woman, New Earth: Sexist Ideologies and Human Liberation* (New York: Seabury Press, 1975). Ruether has never questioned the authenticity of the spiritual quest represented by Goddess religion, but she has clearly had problems with some of the historical conclusions and theological assumptions of Goddess feminists. See, for example, "Female Symbols, Values, and Context," *Christianity and Crisis* 47 (1987): 460–64, and "A Religion for Women: Sources and Strategies," *Christianity and Crisis* 39 (1979): 307–11.

5. See Marina Warner, *Alone of All Her Sex* (New York: Simon and Schuster, 1979).

6. My reading of some of the Marian literature in a more feminist light can be found in *New Catholic Women*, chapter 6.

7. Merlin Stone, *When God Was a Woman* (New York: Dial Press, 1976), and *Ancient Mirrors of Womanhood: A Treasury of Goddess and Heroine Folklore from around the World* (Boston: Beacon Press, 1979, 1984).

8. Stone's work postulated an ancient matriarchy where women held religious and political power and ruled over an essentially biophilic world. That world came to an end, she says, when hostile Semites, committed to the religion of Yahweh and to the destruction of all other religious systems, conquered and destroyed female communities. It is an easy step to connect patriarchy and all its ills to the Jews, a step that Jewish feminists have been especially sensitive to. See Judith Plaskow, "Christian Feminism and Anti-Judaism," *Cross Currents* 28 (1978): 306–9. This essay was republished as "Blaming Jews for Inventing Patriarchy" and printed with Annette Daum's "Blaming Jews for the Death of the Goddess" in *Lilith* 7 (1980): 7–12.

9. Carol P. Christ, "The New Feminist Theology: A Review of the Literature," *Religious Studies Review* 3 (1977): 203–12.

10. Penelope Washbourn, "Becoming Woman: Menstruation as a Spiritual Experience," and Carol P. Christ, "Why Women Need the Goddess," can both be found in *Womanspirit Rising*, ed. Judith Plaskow and Carol P. Christ (San Francisco: Harper and Row, 1979).

11. Naomi Goldenberg, *The Changing of the Gods* (Boston: Beacon Press, 1979), and Elaine Pagels, *The Gnostic Gospels* (New York: Random House, 1979).

12. Charlene Spretnak, *The Politics of Women's Spirituality: Essays on the Rise of Spiritual Power within the Feminist Movement* (New York: Doubleday, 1982).

13. Rosemary Ruether, "A Religion for Women: Sources and Strategies" (cited note 4), p. 307. Ruether's argument that one must renew from within the tradition does *not* mean that one must renew from within the Christian tradition, or that the Christian tradition is the only valid one. All of her articles on witchcraft and Goddess religion have stated her belief that she has no problem with people exploring paganism as a religious alternative. Her concern is that Goddess feminists apply the same critical yardsticks to paganism as they do to other religions. Furthermore, Ruether does not argue that people must stay within the tradition into which they were born: she has been consistently supportive of exploring other options. At the same time, she insists that feminist interpreters treat *all* religious traditions with integrity, noting the good and bad aspects of each.

14. Again, Ruether does *not* mean that Christianity is the only true religion. On the contrary, her work starts with the presupposition that true religious experience is available to all peoples in all cultures. The rejection of Christianity in favor of another religion presents no problem to her. Ruether's criticisms of Goddess religion are directed toward its uses of its own sources. Since all religions—including those with goddesses—have been shaped by patriarchy in some way, she argues, one needs to examine the sources critically and to look carefully before leaping to the conclusion that Goddess religion is an adumbration of feminism. *Gaia and God* (chapter 1, note 18) makes her case comprehensively.

15. Carol P. Christ, *The Laughter of Aphrodite: Reflections on a Journey to the Goddess* (San Francisco: Harper and Row, 1987), p. 61.

16. Ibid.

17. Rosemary Ruether, "Goddesses and Witches: Liberation and Countercultural Feminism," *Christian Century* 97 (1980): 842–47.

18. Adrienne Rich, "Natural Resources," in *The Dream of a Common Language* (New York: W. W. Norton, 1987), p. 67.

19. Judith Ochshorn, *Female Experience and the Nature of the Divine* (Bloomington: Indiana University Press, 1981).

20. Christ, *The Laughter of Aphrodite*, p. 162.

21. Ibid., p. xi.

22. Anne Carr, *Transforming Grace* (San Francisco: Harper and Row, 1988).

23. See above, chapter 1, note 16.

24. Christ, *The Laughter of Aphrodite*, p. xi.

25. See, for example, Gordon Kaufman, "Nuclear Eschatology and the Study of Religion," *Journal of the American Academy of Religion* 51 (1983): 3–14. Kaufman, taking an apocalyptic view of the contemporary situation, says, "We must be prepared to enter into the most radical kind of deconstruction and reconstruction of the traditions we have inherited, including especially the most central and precious symbols" (p. 13).

26. William James, *The Varieties of Religious Experience* (1902; New York: New American Library, 1958), p. 328.

27. Starhawk, *Truth or Dare: Encounters with Power and Authority* (San Francisco: Harper and Row, 1987).

28. Eisler, *The Chalice and the Blade*, p. 164.

29. Mary Wakeman, "Ancient Sumer and the Women's Movement: The Process of Reaching Behind, Encompassing and Going Beyond," *Journal of Feminist Studies in Religion* 1.2 (1985): 25.

30. Ibid., p. 26.

Chapter 6. Spiritual Work

1. To see how someone uses actual motherhood experience to construct a spirituality for women, see Carol Ochs, *Women and Spirituality* (Totowa, N.J.: Rowman and Allanheld, 1983).

2. For a brilliant analysis of the differences between the spiritual imaginations of men and women in the Middle Ages, especially in relation to the motherhood of God, see Carolyn Walker Bynum, *Jesus as Mother: Studies in the Spirituality of the High Middle Ages* (Berkeley: University of California Press, 1982).

3. Two books unrelated to spirituality are helpful here. Mary Catherine Bateson, *Composing a Life* (New York: Atlantic Monthly Press, 1989), shows how women create their lives and themselves often improvisationally. Carolyn Heilbrun's *Writing a Woman's Life* (New York: Ballantine Books, 1988) explains from the perspective of literary biography why women must turn to one another for stories and life scripts that help them to get beyond the limitations set for them by their socialization.

4. Francis Thompson, "The Hound of Heaven," in *The Poems of Francis Thompson* (London: Oxford University Press, 1941), p. 89.

5. Blaise Pascal, the seventeenth-century philosopher whose Jansenist spirituality tended to be somewhat gloomy, once remarked that the problem with the world is that people are afraid to stay alone in their rooms. For

a reflection on desire and the fear of solitude, see Luther Askeland, "The God in the Moment," *Cross Currents* 40 (1990–91): 457–76.

6. Again, the best book on Augustine's spiritual journey is Peter Brown, *Augustine of Hippo* (chapter 1, note 17). Brown takes care to show how Augustine both longed for worldly success and found himself unable to accept its lure once he recognized that the object of his desire was God. All that Augustine dreamed for in terms of personal success was relinquished so that he could pursue what he knew to be an unattainable goal.

7. I still find the best translation of the *Comedy* to be that of Dorothy L. Sayers, published by Penguin Books. Her notes are excellent and are also a good introduction to medieval thought. For more extensive explanations of the realities of sin, see her essay "The Meaning of Heaven and Hell" in her book *Introductory Papers on Dante* (London: Methuen and Co., 1954), pp. 44–72.

8. Sayers makes great use of the writing of Charles Williams in her notes and introductions to Dante. Williams was himself drawn in particular to the theology of romantic love in Dante. For an introduction to Williams and his vision of spiritual growth grounded in human love, see Mary McDermott Schideler, *The Theology of Romantic Love: A Study of the Writings of Charles Williams* (Grand Rapids: W. S. Eerdmans, 1980).

9. In an effort to explore different dimensions of the divine/human interaction, I sometimes read through old litanies, classical lists of names and attributes for Christ, Mary, and the saints. In reflecting on the "Litany of the Blessed Virgin Mary," I was struck by the power of her various titles and epiphanies. Feminist interpreters have made connections between the attributes of Mary and various traits of ancient goddesses, and many women have been led closer to the Goddess because of those affinities. An interesting new book that leads its author closer to *Mary* because of those associations is China Galland's *Longing for Darkness: Tara and the Black Madonna* (London: Penguin Books, 1990).

10. Thomas Berry, "The Dream of the Earth: Our Way to the Future," *Cross Currents* 37 (1987): 217.

11. One can consider some arenas of peace and justice work like Amnesty International or Pax Christi International, or local groups like county soup kitchens or shelters. A relatively new group that collects money from women to be used *for* women is Mary's Pence. Information about them can be obtained from P.O. Box 29078, Chicago, Ill. 60629.

12. J. D. Salinger, *Franny and Zooey* (New York: Bantam Books, 1964), and R. M. French, trans., *The Way of the Pilgrim* (1930; New York: Seabury Press, 1965).

13. Teresa of Avila, *The Interior Castle*, 1.10, in *The Collected Works of Teresa of Avila*, ed. Kieran Kavanaugh, O.C.D., and Otilio Rodriguez, O.C.D. (Washington, D.C.: Institute of Carmelite Studies, 1980), 2:303.

Epilogue

1. Vincent McNabb was a Jesuit priest who was famous in England in the early part of the twentieth-century Catholic revival. He was a brilliant preacher, teacher, and writer and was remembered often for his witty remarks. Whether this one is true or apocryphal, I do not know.

2. As related in Alma Lutz, *Created Equal* (New York: John Day, 1940), pp. 11–12.

3. See Mary Daly, "The Women's Movement: An Exodus Community," *Religious Education* 67 (1972): 327–33.